the Wrestling Drill Book

BILL WELKER

EDITOR

Human Kinetics

Library of Congress Cataloging-in-Publication Data

The wrestling drill book / Bill Welker, editor.

   p. cm.

  ISBN 0-7360-5460-X (soft cover)

 1. Wrestling--Training. I. Welker, Bill, 1947-

  GV1196.4.T7W74 2005

  796.812--dc22

                  2005014088

ISBN-10: 0-7360-5460-X

ISBN-13: 978-0-7360-5460-7

Acquisitions Editor: Jason Muzinic; **Developmental Editors:** Jennifer L. Walker and Kase Johnstun; **Assistant Editor:** Mandy Maiden; **Copyeditor:** Jacqueline Eaton Blakely; **Proofreader:** Andrew Smith; **Graphic Designer:** Bob Reuther; **Graphic Artist:** Sandra Meier; **Photo Manager:** Dan Wendt; **Cover Designer:** Keith Blomberg; **Photographer (interior):** Mark Anderman; photos on pages 1, 31, 85, 115, 153, 177, and 231 courtesy *Wrestling Magazine*; **Printer:** Sheridan Books

We thank Oak Glen High School in New Cumberland, West Virginia, for assistance in providing the location for the photo shoot for this book.

Human Kinetics books are available at special discounts for bulk purchase. Special editions or book excerpts can also be created to specification. For details, contact the Special Sales Manager at Human Kinetics.

Printed in the United States of America

10 9 8 7 6 5 4 3 2

Human Kinetics
Web site: www.HumanKinetics.com

United States: Human Kinetics
P.O. Box 5076
Champaign, IL 61825-5076
800-747-4457
e-mail: humank@hkusa.com

Canada: Human Kinetics
475 Devonshire Road Unit 100
Windsor, ON N8Y 2L5
800-465-7301 (in Canada only)
e-mail: orders@hkcanada.com

Europe: Human Kinetics
107 Bradford Road
Stanningley
Leeds LS28 6AT, United Kingdom
+44 (0) 113 255 5665
e-mail: hk@hkeurope.com

Australia: Human Kinetics
57A Price Avenue
Lower Mitcham, South Australia 5062
08 8277 1555
e-mail: liaw@hkaustralia.com

New Zealand: Human Kinetics
Division of Sports Distributors NZ Ltd.
P.O. Box 300 226 Albany
North Shore City
Auckland
0064 9 448 1207
e-mail: info@humankinetics.co.nz

This book is dedicated to Coach Mal Paul and Coach Lyman "Beans" Weaver. These men knew the significance of drill work for producing championship teams and wrestlers. As coaches, they not only developed athletes but also molded boys into men, epitomizing the essence of integrity, hard work, and perseverance. Coach Paul and Coach Weaver have since been inducted into the National Wrestling Hall of Fame from the Pennsylvania Chapter.

Mal Paul
Head wrestling coach
Shamokin High School
1946-1965

Lyman "Beans" Weaver
Assistant wrestling coach
Shamokin High School
1950-1965

Contents

Drill Finder

Key

Drill level of difficulty: N = Novice; I = Intermediate; A = Advanced
Drill category: S=Solitary; P=Partner

Foreword

The Wrestling Drill Book is unique in that it assists coaches from the youth to college levels to develop championship wrestlers by teaching the basics. We often forget that it is the simple foundations of a sport that produce winning programs and contestants.

Some of the best high school and collegiate coaches in the nation were selected as chapter authors. These coaches developed their chapters in a sequential manner, moving from simple to more complex drills. Both initial and counter drills are stressed in each of the first five chapters, with chapter 6 offering a plethora of conditioning drills.

There are no fancy "clinic" drills. The book allows all coaches to choose those drills that are appropriate to their wrestlers' abilities and needs. Furthermore, each phase of wrestling includes drills that are easy to understand, teach, and, ultimately, perform.

The final chapter adds structure to drill work and well beyond. The editor, Bill Welker, shares his five decades of experience as a competitor, coach, and official. He reveals basic practice outlines, workout formats, motivational methods, and yearlong strategies for developing championship wrestling programs. It is like having a coaches' handbook to support dynamic drill instruction.

You will find *The Wrestling Drill Book* a must-read no matter what level of the sport you coach. You made a very wise choice.

Bobby Douglas
Head wrestling coach
Iowa State University

Acknowledgments

I would like to take this opportunity to thank every one of the coaches who made *The Wrestling Drill Book* a reality. I also want to thank Mike Dyer, strength and conditioning coach at Rocky Mountain High School (Colorado).

Special note of appreciation is forwarded to the models—Ronnell Green, Joel Timmons, Abby Rush, Cody Miller, Ronnie Green, and Bryce Rush—for their dedicated efforts during the photo sessions. Also, gratitude is extended to the administration and Coach Larry Shaw for the use of their mat room at Oak Glen High School (West Virginia). Coach Shaw's additional expertise was greatly appreciated, along with Coach Buzz Evans of Wheeling Park High School (West Virginia).

A note of thanks to Andrew R. Welker for his technological support. Likewise, appreciation is expressed to Mark Anderman, the freelance photographer for this book, for his undaunted patience. A special thank-you to my friends, the late Coach Joseph J. Thomas and the late Sgt. Mark J. Gerrity, USMC, men who cherished every aspect of the sport of wrestling.

I also want to thank Human Kinetics staff members Ted Miller, Ed McNeely, Jason Muzinic, Jennifer Walker, Kase Johnstun, Sue Outlaw, Jennifer Altstadt, Mandy Maiden, and Cathy Gundrum for their professionalism throughout the development of this book.

Finally, a loving thank-you to my wife, Peggy, for her words of encouragement and patience from the beginning to the conclusion of this writing project.

Introduction: The Purpose

The reality has been and will always remain the same: Champions are made in the practice room. The prime ingredient is *drill, drill, drill* during every wrestling workout session. This creates something akin to that elusive realm known as athletic perfection.

Without move perfection in wrestling, the wrestler who must think before reacting is lost. One high school wrestling coach put it bluntly: "If I have to yell at you what to do during a match, it's too late. That's why the hell we drill."

Unfortunately, should such drill engagement be disorganized and not based on successful practice or experience, the wrestlers will gain nothing from the endeavor except bad habits. Sometimes, practice makes permanent, not perfect.

The purpose of this instructional book is to expose you to wrestling drills in a systematic order that have been proven advantageous via the test of time. They are founded on the basics of the mat sport. The wrestling drills are primarily geared toward coaches at the high school and college levels. However, these drills would be very beneficial to junior high and middle school and youth coaches as well.

As the editor of this book, Bill Welker was determined to create a wrestling resource that would assist all scholastic coaches in producing championship-caliber wrestlers.

The drills described in the ensuing chapters are based on the importance of proper hip positioning (or center of gravity) in all facets of wrestling. It is a fundamental aspect of the mat sport often overlooked by coaches. Also, the drills are presented in a manner that leads the participants to the "big picture" of actual wrestling.

Chapter 1 concentrates on essential movement drills in the areas of takedowns, escapes and reversals, and riding and pinning combinations. The reader will also be exposed to essential counter drills for the various initial drills demonstrated. Bill Archer, chapter 1 contributor, will walk you through every step.

Chapters 2 through 5 illustrate both skill and corresponding counter skill drills to actual moves. The emphasis in these chapters is on takedowns, escapes, reversals, rides, and pinning combinations. This approach clearly promotes wrestler awareness of how wrestling is a sport composed of a relationship between moves and countermoves. Dave LaMotte, Pat Pecora, Ed Peery, Jim Akerly, and Craig Turnbull are the contributors who brilliantly display these important practice drills.

Chapter 6 presents significant conditioning drills. They include strength, endurance, cardiovascular enhancement, and flexibility drills. Their purpose is twofold in nature. First, they assist in developing wrestler conditioning. And second, they prepare the wrestler for live-action wrestling. Coach Ken Taylor does an outstanding job illustrating how important these conditioning drills are to producing championship wrestlers.

Chapter 7 was written by the editor, Dr. William A. "Bill" Welker, who has been an active participant in scholastic wrestling for 50 years as a competitor, coach, official, and author. Chapter 7 offers a yearlong workout road map for dedicated coaches and wrestlers that begins with discussing pre- and in-season practices. It also examines such significant topics as instruction on new moves, organized drill formats, wrestler staleness, and coaching enthusiasm. The author introduces coaches to various specialized wrestling workouts: chain wrestling, situation wrestling, round-robin wrestling, and blindfold wrestling. He concludes by suggesting numerous off-season activities, such as running, weightlifting, and other sport endeavors, that will further assist in promoting wrestling endurance and movement skills.

The drills emphasized in this wrestling reference book have been developed and utilized by ultrasuccessful coaches for decades throughout the country. They work because they are grounded on sound principles of wrestling.

As a responsible and dedicated coach, you know the level of knowledge and ability of the wrestlers under your charge. The format of this book allows you to choose those drills that would be the most beneficial for your mat sport competitors.

Everyone knows that the fundamentals (or essentials) breed champions and winning teams in all sports at every level of competition. *The Wrestling Drill Book* offers such a back-to-basics approach and will guide you in that direction.

Essential Movement Drills

Bill Archer

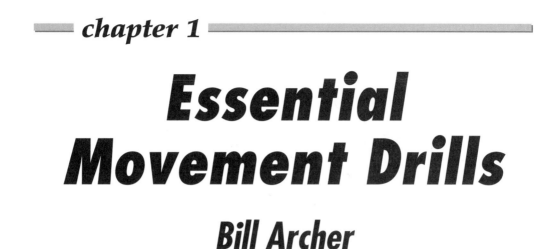

Accept the challenges, so that you may feel the exhilaration of victory.

General George S. Patton

Wrestling, like most sports, is a competition made up of movements and involving the starting and stopping of motion. During the infancy of wrestling in America, coaches taught holds; today, coaches teach *moves,* or *essential movements.*

Essential movements in wrestling need to be drilled correctly and repeatedly in order for the wrestler to experience success during competition. Thus, the structure of drills must be such that the essential skills develop the ability to execute moves naturally.

The coaches' and wrestlers' attitude toward the drilling process is of paramount importance. To let the wrestlers slowly and thoughtlessly go through the motions makes the drills lose much of their value. The coaches and wrestlers must perform drill work as closely to live wrestling as possible.

The following movement drills are intended to prepare wrestlers for those drills that promote perfection of techniques in all areas of wrestling. With the successful completion of movement drills, the wrestlers are better prepared for and have a deeper understanding of proper movement when practicing drills in all facets of the sport. Introduce these movement drills at the beginning of the wrestling season. In the following movement drills and the drills throughout the rest of the book, wrestler 1 and wrestler 2 will be referred to as W1 and W2.

Movement Drills in Neutral Position

There is no area in wrestling more important than the neutral position; matches are often won or lost in this area. It is imperative that the coach place significant emphasis on movement drills in the neutral position. If a wrestler is weak on his feet, he will be at a disadvantage during the rigors of competition.

Stance

An essential wrestling stance must be both offensive and defensive in nature. In this position a wrestler can quickly adjust to changing situations and is prepared to attack or to defend his opponent's attack.

Emphasize the following fundamentals of stance and movement:

1. Beware of extreme positions. For example, the wrestlers must always attempt to keep their feet no more than shoulder-width apart for sound balance. Also, the wrestlers need to position their elbows in front of their bodies, slightly bent toward each other. This prevents the wrestlers' opponents from gaining inside control.

2. Keep compact with a low center of gravity.

3. Never cross your feet.

4. Tuck your head, facing the opponent's midsection.

5. Keep elbows against the body and palms facing each other.

6. Take small steps, except when attacking.

The following drills prepare the wrestlers to hone skills related to a solid and defensive stance.

1 CHANGING LEVEL FOR PENETRATION

Setup

W2 stands with his legs well enough apart so W1 can penetrate through them (*a*). W1 is facing W2 in the neutral stance previously described.

Action

W1 lowers his hips and steps forward toward W2. Next, W1 penetrates through W2's legs, scooting on his hands and knees underneath W2's body (*b*). W1 completes the drill by returning to his original stance facing away from W2 (*c*). Have wrestlers change positions and repeat the drill, continuing to repeat the drill in this reverse-role sequence until you are satisfied with their performance, as with all drills.

Coaching Point

This drill emphasizes the importance of lowering the hips (or center of gravity) before attacking an opponent's legs. It also demonstrates to the wrestlers the significance of penetrating through their opponents, especially when attempting a double-leg takedown.

Setup

W2 holds W1's head on his chest in the standing position (*a*). W1 faces W2 in the basic neutral stance previously described.

Action

W1 penetrates knee-over-toe, grabbing a single leg, driving in, and picking up the leg (*b-c*). He then drops the leg and takes the same shot on the opposite leg.

Coaching Point

The primary purpose of this drill is for the drill wrestler to back up the drill partner with each shot. It also teaches the wrestlers about the importance of giving it that "second effort" when the initial maneuver is unsuccessful in match competition. This drill further assists wrestlers in learning to keep their heads in proper position when performing certain single-leg takedowns.

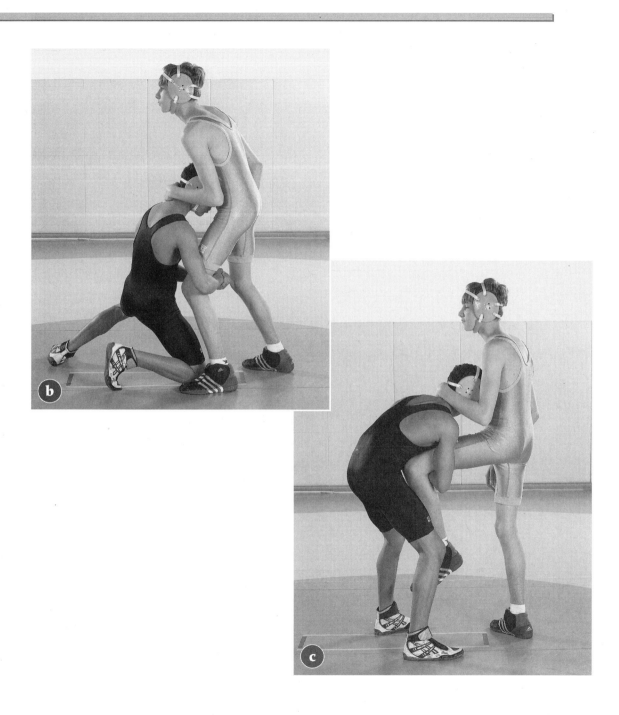

3   SPRAWL-BACK DRILL

Setup
This is a solitary drill in which each wrestler starts in a square stance in the neutral position (*a*).

Action
On the whistle, the wrestler sprawls to the mat, landing on hands and feet with a slight twist of the hips (*b*).

Coaching Point
It is very important to emphasize that the knees not touch the mat when sprawling. The wrestlers must understand that dropping to the knees when sprawling allows their opponents to pull their legs in for the takedown.

PUMMELING

Setup
Both drill partners start from the overhook and underhook position, with the lead leg always on the underhook side. They must also have their knees slightly bent, positioning their heads on their overhook side (*a*).

Action
On the whistle, the wrestlers are constantly attempting the underhook position by digging into their partner's armpit, alternating underhook arms during the drill (*b*). Their heads rotate to the opposite side as they switch from the overhook to the underhook. The wrestlers' feet should also be moving with their upper bodies, the lead foot always on the underhook side.

Coaching Point
This drill emphasizes the importance of inside control when wrestling in the neutral position. It also assists the wrestlers in becoming more aggressive as they work to gain inside control during actual competition.

Setup

The two wrestlers start from the overhook and underhook position (*a*).

Action

As each partner starts to dig in on the overhook side, W1 raises his underhook elbow high, forcing W2's elbow above his shoulder (*b*). The move sets up W1's opportunity for the duck-under. At this point, W1 lowers his hips as he steps behind W2 with his left leg, ducking his head under W2's arm (*c*). W1 finishes the move by coming up behind W2 and locking his hands around W2's body.

Coaching Point

This drill emphasizes the importance of lowering the hips (or center of gravity) before executing the duck-under takedown. Stress the importance of staying tight against an opponent's body when executing the duck-under. Also, stress the need to arch the head back so an opponent cannot reestablish his original arm position, blocking the duck-under maneuver.

Setup

W2 stabilizes his position on his knees and elbows, covering his head. W1, who will perform the Spin Drill, puts his chest on top of W2's back (*a*).

Action

On the whistle, W1 blocks W2's triceps with his near arm in the direction he is spinning (*b*). As he turns the corner, W1 takes short choppy steps. He continues spinning in the same direction until the coach blows the whistle for him to change direction (*c*).

Coaching Point

It is important that the drill wrestler stay off his knees throughout the drill for full mobility.

Movement Drills in Defensive Position

Proper defensive position has been neglected in recent years; coaches should spend more time teaching it. The wrestler with insufficient defensive positioning skills is an easier target to be tilted or pinned.

7   STAND-UP ON THE WALL

Setup
The wrestlers put themselves in the defensive referee's position with the side of their body against the wrestling room wall (*a*).

Action
They then quickly stand up, stepping with their outside leg and placing their back against the wall. Their upper legs should be parallel to the mat (*b*).

Coaching Point
This drill promotes stand-up quickness and proper positioning after the stand-up.

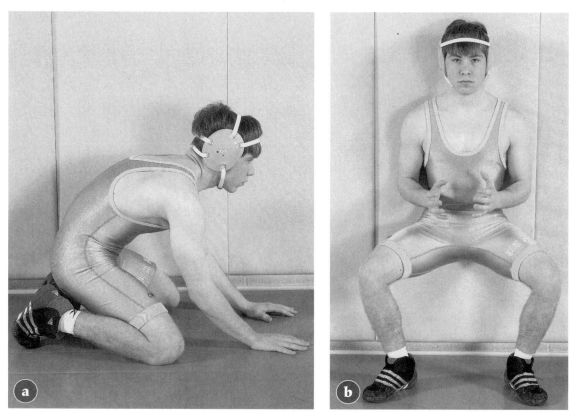

Setup

W1 and W2 are in the referee's position (*a*).

Action

On the whistle, W1 must avoid being forced down to the mat. During the drill, W1 spreads his base and goes to both his elbows and hands, while W2 attempts to drive him off his base (*b*).

Coaching Point

Stress to the wrestlers that they must not drop to the abdomen because that is when the opponent can turn them onto their backs.

Setup

In this drill, W2 starts in the spiral ride position, with his right hand locked inside W1's far leg and left arm across W1's upper chest. W1 is in the basic defensive referee's position (*a*).

Action

On the whistle, W1 scoots his inside knee away and pushes his back against W2's chest. W1 then raises his outside leg to place his foot on the mat. At the same time, W1 isolates W2's inside hand with both his hands (*b*). W1 extends W2's inside hand away from his body, while driving off his front foot to a standing position to set up his escape (*c*).

Coaching Point

Emphasize the significance of quickness and hand control when standing up. Stress that the defensive wrestler keep his back perpendicular to the mat prior to standing up.

Setup
W2 assumes the defensive referee's position. W1 then leans his back against W2's side in a crouching position (*a*).

Action
On the coach's signal, W1 raises his right arm and leg to set up his cut-away (*b*). Finally, W1 turns to his left and pushes away, facing W2 (*c*). The drill is repeated, using the left arm and leg before the wrestlers reverse drill positions.

Coaching Point
Stress the importance of the quick push-away when securing the escape maneuver.

Setup

W1 starts on the bottom in the referee's position. W2 is in the conventional offensive referee's position.

Action

W1 starts the drill by crossing his inside hand over the outside hand (*a*). He then sits through and reaches back for inside W2's near leg. At this point, W2 keeps his hand inside W1's leg (*b*). While W1 comes around and behind, W2 reswitches (*c-d*).

Coaching Point

The drill should last approximately 10 to 15 seconds. Emphasize leg control for both wrestlers when switching and reswitching. Note: Beginners have a tendency to reach over their opponents' backs when switching.

Setup

This is a solitary drill in which each wrestler starts with his head and knees on the mat and hands on his hips.

Action

In this position, each wrestler rolls on his upper shoulders and elbows one direction, pushing off his toes (*a*), and then changes direction on the sound of the whistle (*b*). This solitary drill can last 15 to 30 seconds.

Coaching Point

The purpose of this drill is to teach the wrestlers to roll on the top of their shoulders rather than the middle of the back, which is a bad habit that must be stopped. The drill also prepares wrestlers for the Granby-roll series.

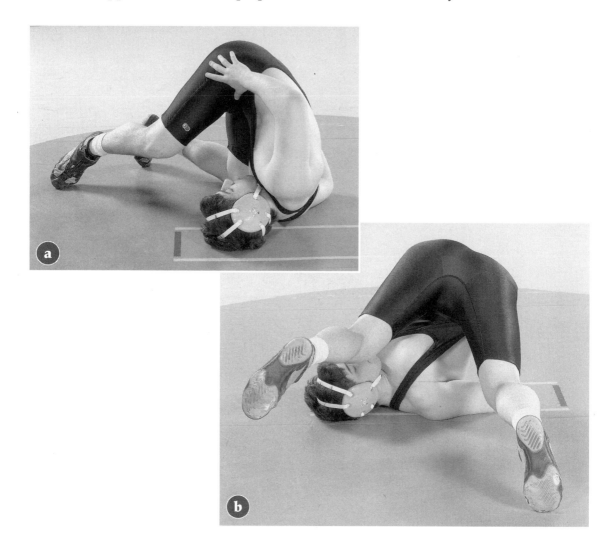

Movement Drills in Offensive Position

The primary goal in the offensive position is to score a fall. This cannot be accomplished if a wrestler is weak in the ability to ride his opponent. Movement drills in the offensive position can aid the wrestler in perfecting riding and pinning skills.

13   SCRAMBLING

Setup
The coach places W1 in any unusual position pressing against W2 and facing away from W2.

Action
On the whistle, W2 can move in any direction. It is the responsibility of W1 to quickly adjust his body to be in proper riding position. In doing so, W1 should first attack W2's lower-back area prior to securing a proper ride of his choosing.

Coaching Point
This drill prepares the offensive wrestler to react to the unexpected at any time during the match. You can vary the drill by telling the offensive wrestler he cannot grab the ankle, ride the legs, or use a tight waist. This is a unique approach to entice the offensive wrestler to initiate alternative breakdowns.

Setup
W2 is in the bottom referee's position with W1 on top on his feet behind W2 and his hands on W2's hips.

Action
On the whistle, W2 continuously sits out and turns in or moves forward. W1's responsibility is to keep a firm hold on the hips while maneuvering on his feet and staying behind W2.

Coaching Point
The purpose of this drill is to teach the wrestlers to ride behind an opponent by not riding too high, staying on the opponent's hips. A variation of this drill is to have the offensive wrestler place his chest on the defensive wrestler's lower back with his hands on the defensive wrestler's hips. They then perform the same drill movements. The offensive wrestler's goal is to keep his chest on the defensive wrestler's lower back.

LIFT AND RETURN

Setup

The wrestlers are standing, with W1 in control behind W2 with his hands locked together in the clap position, left hand over right hand (*a*).

Action

W1 steps to the side, bending his knees to a squat position (*b*). Next, W1 lifts W2 off the mat, bringing his right knee up (*c*). This turns W2 parallel to the mat. As W2 is returned to the mat, landing on his side, W1 simultaneously drops to both knees and unlocks his hands.

Coaching Point

This breakdown drill teaches wrestlers to correctly and safely return the opponent to the mat from the standing position.

Setup

The wrestlers start in the spiral ride position (*a*).

Action

W1, rotating counterclockwise, pulls W2 to his near hip and quickly slides his right arm over W2's top leg and under W2's bottom leg. W1 also has his right arm bent with his elbow touching the mat (*b*). At this point, W2's legs are lifted by W1, who rests his elbow on his lap as he steps up (*c*). W1 completes the drill by stacking W2 on his back by driving him forward (*d*).

Coaching Point

This drill teaches the wrestlers to move from the spiral ride position to a pinning situation as quickly as possible. Point out the importance of the offensive wrestler keeping his head in front of the defensive wrestler when the Navy is secured.

17 SPIRAL RIDE TO HOOK AND PIN

Setup
The wrestlers start in the spiral ride position (*a*).

Action
W1 pulls W2 to his near hip while hooking his top arm (*b*). He then starts pulling W2 to his back. W1 finishes the drill by overhooking W2's head and pressing his shoulders to the mat (*c*).

Coaching Point
This drill teaches the wrestlers to move from the spiral ride position to another pinning situation. Far too often wrestlers do not follow through with successful ride techniques and risk being warned or penalized for stalling.

Conclusion

Essential movements, or what some call the basics, are so important in preparing athletes to deal with the rigors of wrestling. The preceding drills are just the beginning of a journey toward developing championship wrestlers, which will involve even more and more drill work on the mats. As the coach, you must continue to stress to your athletes the significance of repeatedly practicing moves. Essential movement drills are necessary for perfecting all wrestling maneuvers.

Wrestling is a very complex sport. There are a number of areas that must be taught by the coach and learned by the wrestlers. Failing to do so will lead to a less than successful wrestling program.

Essential movement drills are stepping stones that prepare the wrestler to properly perform takedown, escape and reversal, riding, and pinning combination drills. Think of the essential movement drills as prerequisites to the many success-oriented drills you will be exposed to in the remaining chapters of this book.

chapter 2

Takedown Drills

Dave LaMotte

*If you want a place in the sun,
you've got to put up with a few blisters.*
Abigail Van Buren

The objective in wrestling is to score a fall. When wrestlers are aggressively pursuing the fall, it makes the action in the match a lot more exciting for the fans. However, the more accomplished and experienced the wrestlers are, the more difficult it becomes to secure a fall. This is why the perfection of takedown skills in wrestling is the first step toward becoming a champion wrestler.

No student of the mat sport would disagree with the premise that takedowns are the name of the game in wrestling. In fact, it has been statistically proven that the wrestler who scores the first takedown usually wins the match (about 85 percent of the time).

Thus, the beginning of your season (after a proper conditioning period) should be devoted primarily to takedown instruction. It has always been my contention that 70 percent of drill work before the competitive phase of the program should concentrate on takedowns. By midseason, wrestlers should spend about 50 percent of their practice time on their feet.

The components of takedown wrestling often take more time to cultivate than mat wrestling. To have success in this area, a basic philosophy of attacking and counterattacking must be developed and followed. A good takedown wrestler must be able to move his feet gracefully while constantly maintaining a good base (or center of gravity) and to step in and penetrate his opponent's defenses.

At the same time, the wrestler must know instinctively how to finish the attack and be prepared to defend all types of attacks executed by his opponent. Thus, the drills in this chapter focus on controlling and clearing the tie-up position for offensive takedown attacks and basic defensive counterattacks and strategies.

Takedown Drills

These drills are for close-contact wrestling and are designed to teach reaction maneuvers when the opponent puts "hands on" or moves out of position. The wrestler performing the drill should always start with his head up, hips (center of gravity) down, elbows in, and knees bent. In every drill, each wrestler takes turns being the drill partner.

Setup

W1 shoots a single-leg when W2 reaches for W1 (*a-b*).

Action

W2's responsibility is to sprawl back so that W1 must switch from a single-leg to double before driving W2 to the mat (*c*). W1 must change to a double as quickly as possible.

Coaching Point

The emphasis of these drills is to promote the importance of lowering the hips and penetrating the opponent's defense. The wrestlers must learn to react to the opponent's change of stance by changing attack from single-leg to double-leg immediately.

(continued)

Setup

W1 starts with a double-leg position on W2 as he reaches for W1 (*a*).

Action

As W2 sprawls back, W1 lifts W2's right leg up as he drives his head into W2's side (*b*). W1 continues driving his head into W2's side. At the same time, W1 blocks W2's left leg with his right arm. W1 finishes the double takedown by lifting W2's leg higher while forcing W2's body to the side with his head and driving W2 to the mat (*c*).

Coaching Point

Emphasize the importance of the offensive wrestler lifting the defensive wrestler's leg as high as possible while using his head to assist in driving the defensive wrestler to the side before taking him to the mat. The offensive wrestler cannot hesitate when executing this highly effective takedown.

(continued)

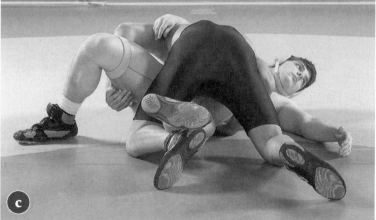

Setup

W1 starts with a double-leg on W2 (*a*).

Action

W1 loses control of W2's right leg as W2 sprawls his leg away. W1 then attacks W2's left leg with his right arm while grasping his right wrist with his left hand (*b*). In this position, W1 can either turn the corner and drive through W2, capturing his far knee, or W1 can quickly stand up, controlling W2's leg, before performing the single-leg takedown.

Coaching Point

The importance of this situation drill is to teach adjusting position from the double-leg, changing to a single-leg attack. Keep the wrestlers aware of this point so they learn to change tactics when appropriate.

(continued)

Setup
W1 positions his right ear on the back of W2's spine. His left arm goes deep through the back of W2's crotch while his right hand grips under the left arm toward the back (*a*).

Action
W1 then squats in good position and explodes up to lift W2 off the mat (*b*). W1 repeats the drill several times on both sides of the partner's body.

Coaching Point
This drill teaches the proper technique for lifting an opponent off the mat. You must always stress this point.

Setup

W2 reaches for W1 in the neutral position (*a*).

Action

W1 deeply penetrates W2's defenses, hooking W2's right leg with his left leg while shooting the double-leg takedown (*b*). As they drop to the mat, W1 quickly releases his arms around W2's legs as he prepares to adjust to a ride or pinning combination (*c*).

Coaching Point

The wrestlers must be taught not to allow their upper body to trail their trip leg or they will be placed in an off-balance position. Emphasis should also be on whipping their trip leg back as they shoulder drive through their opponents for the double-leg takedown.

DOUBLE-LEG DRIVE-THROUGH WHEN OPPONENT REACHES

Setup

W1 is in proper attack position when W2 reaches or rises up out of proper neutral position for defending a takedown (*a*).

Action

W1 quickly lowers his center of gravity and penetrates into W2's hips, grasping behind his knees (*b*). W1 finishes the drill by driving through W2, bringing him to the mat (*c*).

Coaching Point

The wrestlers must learn to react quickly for the takedown when an opponent places himself out of proper position and reaches in the neutral position.

24

INSIDE ARM-DRAG
TO DOUBLE-LEG DRIVE-THROUGH DRILL

Setup

W2 grabs W1's wrist on the trail-leg side (*a*).

Action

W1 rotates his wrist inward and downward across his body. He also grabs above W2's elbow, completing the arm-drag and stepping into the double-leg drive-through position (*b-c*).

Coaching Point

The wrestlers must understand the need to tightly control the opponent's arm above the elbow when committing to the inside arm-drag while shooting the double-leg.

25

OUTSIDE ARM-DRAG
TO DOUBLE-LEG DRIVE-THROUGH

Setup

W2 makes contact by using a collar tie-up on W1's trail-leg side.

Action

W1 then controls the collar tie-up elbow and his other hand grasps W2's far wrist (*a*). W1 then steps back, rolling W2's elbow and wrist off his head. At the same time, W1 drags W2's arm across and between both of their bodies toward W2's far knee (*b*). W1 shoots through W2 for the double-leg takedown (*c-d*).

Coaching Point

Always emphasize the importance of arm control for scoring an arm-drag takedown.

26

ELBOW PULL AND INSIDE SINGLE-LEG
TO DOUBLE-LEG DRIVE-THROUGH

Setup
W2 controls the collar and attempts to snap down W1 (*a*).

Action
W1 then lifts W2's elbow over his shoulder, shooting an inside single-leg (*b*). As W2 sprawls, W1 switches off to a double-leg drive-through takedown (*c-d*).

Coaching Point

As always, emphasize the importance of penetrating or driving through an opponent to score the double-leg takedown.

27 ELBOW BLOCK TO DOUBLE-LEG DRIVE-THROUGH

Setup
W2 places his hand on W1's shoulder (*a*).

Action
W1 goes into motion, driving off his trail leg. W1 uses the elbow-block technique with his thumb inside of W2's elbow when he pops W2's elbow up (*b*). At the same time, W1 lowers his level (center of gravity), makes the step between W2's feet, and executes the double-leg (*c*).

Coaching Point
This drill continues to promote the importance of changing hip position (lowering the center of gravity) in order to penetrate an opponent for the takedown. It also stresses the point of taking advantage of an opponent's mistake with quick-reaction skills.

Setup

W2 is in the collar-tie position.

Action

W1 controls the elbow of W2's collar-tie arm and pulls the elbow from his shoulder while grabbing his opposite wrist (*a*). W1 then lowers his center of gravity, wrapping his arms around W2's leg on the side in which W2 had the collar tie (*b*). He then controls the leg by lifting it high and driving W2 backward to the mat (*c-d*).

Coaching Point

Wrist control and lowering the center of gravity (hips) are essential factors in executing this drill.

Setup

W2 uses a collar tie on W1's lead-leg side, while W1 controls W2's opposite wrist (*a*).

Action

W1 shrugs his shoulder and drives W2's head down while grabbing his collar-tie wrist to force it off his neck (*b*). At the same time, W1 drives W2's head down to the mat for the takedown (*c-d*).

Coaching Point

Wrist control and shoulder shrug quickness must be stressed during this drill.

Setup

W2 underhooks W1 on his lead-leg side (*a*).

Action

W1 immediately forces the underhook elbow inward. As W2 pushes his elbow out, W1 lowers his center of gravity and shoots between the legs on his knees, wrapping his free arm around W2's leg on the side where W2 had the

underhook (*b*). Tilting his shoulders away from W2's leg, W1 then whips W2 to the mat, driving his free arm through the air in the same direction for the takedown (*c-d*).

Coaching Point

It is very important that wrestlers control the opponent's underhook arm, tightly grabbing it above the elbow, when performing the Fireman's Carry.

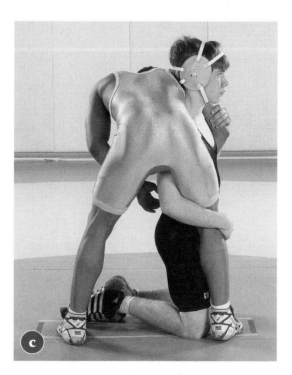

Setup

This takedown drill is a combination of the Fireman's Carry and Elbow Head Pull to Single-Leg (pages 52-53) Drills.

Action

W1 controls W2's underhook in the same manner as in the Fireman's Carry Drill while grabbing the far wrist (*a*). Stepping to the outside of the opposite leg as in a single-leg attack, W1 pulls W2's arm across his body and sweeps in for a single-leg on the opposite side around the knee (*b*). Controlling the underhook arm and driving it down, W1 sits through with the leg that is on W2's underhook side to finish the takedown (*c*).

Coaching Point

As with the Fireman's Carry Drill, emphasize a tight grip above the opponent's underhook elbow.

SINGLE-LEG ATTACK FROM OPPONENT'S UNDERHOOK DRILL

Setup
W2 secures an underhook tie-up on the side of W1's lead leg (*a*).

Action
Pummeling the underhook arm and popping it up, W1 lowers his center of gravity while sweeping his arm around W2's lead leg, picking it up and bringing W2 to the mat (*b-c*).

Coaching Point
Highlight the significance of quickly lowering the center of gravity (hips) as the wrestlers single-leg sweep their partners during the drill.

Setup

This drill starts in a situation where W2 is able to elevate W1's elbow with his underhook (*a*).

Action

As W2 elevates W1's elbow, W1 steps between W2's legs and then headlocks and hips his partner to the mat, controlling W2's far arm above the elbow (*b-c*).

Coaching Point

This drill should be taught as a desperation move for a situation in which a match is nearing the end and the wrestler is behind by three or more points. Wrestlers must have a few strategies for this type of situation.

Takedown Counter Drills

The premise for takedown counter drills is to stop your opponent's initial attack and then create a counterattack in which you score. This is best accomplished by keeping in good position with a proper center-of-gravity (hip) location. In other words, do not allow your opponent to feel comfortable in the neutral position when he attempts takedown maneuvers.

Keep in mind that the fundamentals must be taught first, including conventional sprawling drills, proper crossface techniques and hip positioning drills, and whizzer-hip counter drills to double-leg attacks. Also, review all single-leg counter maneuvers when the attack wrestler has control of the leg on or off the mat. Wrestlers must master these grassroots drills before they learn the more advanced takedown counter drills.

The following drill sequence is set up to demonstrate the first line of defense drills, using the hands to prevent your opponent from penetrating to the legs. The second line of defense drills will illustrate techniques used when the opponent is able to penetrate to the legs or body by maneuvering through the first line of defense.

34   SNAP-DOWN REDIRECT DRILL

Setup
This drill is incorporated when the takedown wrestler is able to work his head under his opponent in the process of attacking the legs. W1 controls W2's head with a collar tie with his right arm, establishing wrist control with his left hand and arm (*a*).

Action
As W2 begins his attempt to penetrate W1, W1 snaps his head and elbows to the mat while sprawling back (*b*). Pressing his chest on W2's back, W1 drives W2's head to the mat, blocking W2's right arm (*c*). Finally, W1 spins around W2 for the takedown.

Coaching Point
When the wrestlers sprawl, stress the importance of sprawling on the toes and placing pressure on the opponent's back before spinning around.

Setup

This drill is a replica of the Snap-Down Redirect Drill, except for the reaction by W1. From the collar tie, as W2 attempts to shoot a double-leg, W1 snaps his partner's head down (*a*).

Action

W1 shucks W2's head to the side, driving his collar-tie elbow across the chin, creating an angle to spin behind W2 and score the defensive takedown (*b-d*).

Coaching Point

Emphasize that the wrestlers must use a quick whipping motion during the shuck before spinning behind.

Setup

This counter drill is used when W2 attempts a double-leg from the open position stance (*a*).

Action

W1 reacts by sprawling back, locking his arms around W2's head and shoulder, and lowering his hips (*b*). As W2 is forced to the mat, W1 (with his head under W2's chest) then wraps his arm around W2's leg while circling to his left and forcing W2's head in the same direction (*c*). At the same time, W1 drives into W2 with his head, forcing W2 off his base and scoring the countertakedown (*d*).

Coaching Point

This drill must be performed with proper and assertive circular motion, forcing the opponent's head in the same direction.

Setup

The wrestlers are in the same headlock position as the previous drill.

Action

W1 forces W2's head toward the mat (*a*). As W2 begins to push his head up, W1 shucks, whipping W2's head away from him (*b*). This allows W1 to attack W2's side for the countertakedown (*c*).

Coaching Point

The emphasis in this drill is the importance of proper head pressure before shucking the opponent's head away and attacking the side for the take-down.

Setup

W1 starts from the front headlock counter position.

Action

W1 stays on his toes and forces W2's head to the mat (*a*). After driving W2's head to the mat, W1 reaches for the cross ankle with his left hand, pulling it toward W2's head (*b*). W1 finishes the move by thrusting into W2 and quickly executing an inside-leg cradle (*c*).

Coaching Point

Emphasize the importance of placing pressure on the opponent's ankle when grabbing the cross ankle so he cannot move it when initiating the drill.

DOUBLE-LEG REACTION COUNTER DRILL

Setup

The wrestlers are in the open stance position.

Action

W2 attempts a double-leg and is blocked by W1 (*a*). As W2 adjusts by attempting to regain his original takedown position, W1 immediately reacts with a counterattack double-leg takedown (*b-c*).

Coaching Point

Stress the significance of not only countering but quickly attacking offensively, not being satisfied with just blocking an attack. This is also an opportune time to finish by driving an opponent to his back with a half nelson.

Setup

W2 shoots a double-leg takedown with W1 sprawling and overhooking the near arm to initiate the whizzer (*a*).

Action

W1 initiates the whizzer and pops his hip into W2, driving W2's head toward the mat (*b*). W1 finishes the counter by forcing W2's head to the mat with his free hand while sprawling away and facing W2 (*c*).

Coaching Point

Two points must be stressed when applying the whizzer. First, the whizzer must be driven with force so that the drill wrestler's shoulder is above the drill partner's shoulder. Second, when popping the near hip into the drill partner to break the double-leg grip, the drill wrestler should not prolong the pressure on the drill partner's body because the drill partner could roll through and score the takedown. In other words, pop the hip and quickly release to break the double-leg grip.

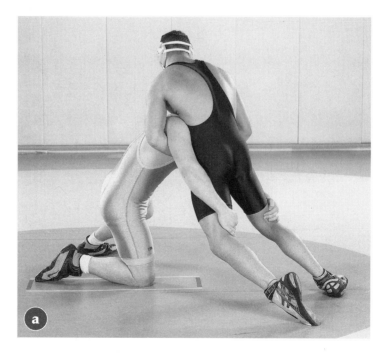

Setup

The purpose of this drill is to teach the wrestlers how to get off their hips when an opponent is close to securing a single takedown. Start the drill with W2 controlling one leg with his head to the outside of W1.

Action

In this position, W1 lifts his outside hip and grabs W2's near-side buttock (*a*). Next, W1 hip-heists his inside leg through while pulling W2's body forward with the buttock hand and posting his free arm on the mat for the counter-score (*b-c*).

Coaching Point

A great prerequisite activity for this counter drill is the Hip-Heist Drill, explained in more detail as a solitary drill in chapter 6 (pages 219-220). It promotes proper technique in executing the hip heist.

Setup

This drill starts with W2 executing a single-leg, lifting it off the mat (*a*).

Action

From this position, W1 must force his head inside, grab W2's outside wrist, and secure a whizzer with his inside arm (*b*). W1 must then work his captured leg to the outside and sprawl it back while driving the whizzer forward and popping his hips into W2 (*c*). W1 can finish the maneuver by forcing W2 to the mat and spinning behind him for the countertakedown.

Coaching Point

The wrestlers must learn to whizzer with pressure while sprawling and forcing the hips into the opponent to succeed in the countertakedown.

43   THE SINGLE-LEG SPLADDLE COUNTER DRILL

Setup
W2 shoots a single-leg takedown with his head inside and on both his knees (*a*).

Action
W1 reacts by pressuring W2's head and back to the mat, stepping his lead foot inside W2's calf, and locking his hands around W2's outside leg (*b*). W1 finishes the counter by dropping to his inside hip and forcing W2's back to the mat for the takedown, near-fall points, and possibly a fall (*c*).

Coaching Point
It is very important that the drill wrestler keep his weight on his lead leg. The drill wrestler must also keep his body pressure on the drill partner so he cannot come to his feet. This weight pressure will also force the drill partner into a ball position, with his head in front of his legs in preparation for the spladdle. After mastering the spladdle, the wrestlers realize the importance of immediately standing up when executing a single-leg to avoid being spladdled.

Conclusion

Developing and using a proper system of takedown drills is the most essential element in becoming a successful takedown artist. The more a skill is repeated correctly, the more firmly it becomes established as an automatic move that is very effective against an opponent.

During competition, action occurs too quickly for the wrestler to stop and think about what to do or how to do it. In wrestling, he who hesitates loses. For this very reason, the wrestler must be willing to invest hours upon hours performing takedown and takedown counter drills.

The bottom line is that to be successful, wrestlers must have the desire to be number one. And that desire to be the best can be fulfilled only with a willingness to drill until a move becomes second nature. That is the premise of this book.

The next three chapters focus on the second phase of the sport—mat or ground wrestling. Starting with chapter 3, you will be introduced to drill tactics in the areas of escapes and reversals, as well as their counters. This is an important area of wrestling that in recent years has been lacking in emphasis; don't allow your wrestlers to overlook it.

Escape and Reversal Drills

Pat Pecora

Let me tell you the secret that has led me to my goal.
My strength lies solely on my tenacity.

Louis Pasteur

With so much emphasis on takedown strategies in recent decades, escape and reversal skills have been given positions of less significance during practice. This contemporary practice has had its negative effects. To the astute observer of mat wrestling, today's wrestlers do not demonstrate the flow of movement in the defensive position needed to assure success.

Today, wrestlers attempt one or two escape or reversal moves in competition, then, if the maneuvers fail, the wrestler stops, and his opponent commences to control him. One vivid example of this problem is the 30-second tiebreaker and how it has changed over the last few years. At the outset, the wrestler who chose the bottom position was very confident of escaping with a quick stand-up. That approach has been compromised.

It is time to again place more importance on the escape-and-reversal defense during the entire match. Wrestlers must be exposed to more drill instruction to improve this area of weakness, and this can be accomplished only on the practice mats.

The following drills are designed to help develop wrestlers' skills in the defensive position. Likewise, you will be exposed to escape and reversal counter drills in the offensive position.

Escape and Reversal Drills

In this section, the drills emphasize the significance of inside control as an important factor for experiencing success in the defensive position. The wrestlers are also taught that a proper base must be established to escape or reverse their opponents.

In coaching wrestling for nearly three decades, I have determined that *inside control* is the first essential principle in escapes and reversals. Inside control is often mistaken for *hand control*, which is a different term. Inside control involves controlling the inside of your body, not just your opponent's hands.

44 INSIDE CONTROL IN THE STANDING POSITION

Setup

The drill begins in a standing position with W2 behind W1.

Action

It is important to be in good position, with W1's head up, back straight, buttocks down, elbows in, and knees bent. During inside control drills, the most important body parts for W1 range from the inside of the elbow up to the armpit. W1 gains inside control of the body by keeping the elbows firmly against his body to stop W2 from getting inside (*a*). (If W2 does get inside, W1 should use a windshield-wiper motion with the arms to regain inside control.) Having gained inside control with the arms, W1 then works on controlling W2's hand or hands (*b*). At this point, W1 cuts and escapes (*c*).

(continued)

Coaching Point

The offensive wrestler's goal is to try to lock his hands around the defensive wrestler's waist or gain wrist control on the defensive wrestler. The defensive wrestler's goal is to get inside control before the offensive wrestler does. If the offensive wrestler gets inside control, start the drill over. With practice, the defensive wrestler should be able to perform this drill with his eyes closed, feeling where the offensive wrestler is at all times. The defensive wrestler must never reach with the hands to get control. This action causes the defensive wrestler's elbows to come out from his body, allowing the offensive wrestler to get inside.

Setup

W1 begins this drill on one knee with W2 behind him.

Action

Again, W1 uses tight inside control and keeps his back perpendicular to the mat (*a*). This drill has the same principles as the previous drill, but in this drill W2 is not allowed to lock his hands in this position. With inside control, W1 then acquires hand control, finishing by pivoting his knee and cutting through for the escape (*b-c*).

(continued)

Coaching Point

It is important that the defensive wrestler not ball up as he is standing so the offensive wrestler cannot cradle him in a real match situation.

46   INSIDE CONTROL ADVANCED DRILLS

Setup

As the year progresses, W1 can add other maneuvers to the "inside control" drills after escaping.

Action

For example, upon escaping, W1 snaps W2 down and spins behind W2, or W1 shoots a double-leg takedown (coach's choice) on W2. That completed, the practice partner would then do the same.

Coaching Point

When an escape has occurred, often the opponent momentarily relaxes. A quick takedown maneuver after an escape is often very effective.

HEAVY DRILLS
WHEN OPPONENT HAS INSIDE CONTROL

Setup
W2 has inside control (hands locked) in the standing position behind W1.

Action
When W2 gains inside control in the standing position, there are two techniques for W1 to make his body "heavy," stopping W2 from bringing W1 to the mat. The first technique involves W1 pushing W2's leg away from his body while W1 forces his own hips away (*a*). The second technique is taught when W2 is up tight against W1's body. If W2's hips are close to W1's hips, W1 locks one of his legs on the outside of W2's leg (*b*).

Coaching Point
Stress that these drills eliminate the offensive wrestler's ability to lift his opponent off the mat. They are easy to teach and very effective for stopping the offensive wrestler from bringing the defensive wrestler to the mat.

48   LAND LIKE A CAT

Setup

W1 is lifted off the mat with W2 behind him. W2 prepares to drive W1 to the mat to W1's side.

Action

If W1 is lifted off the mat, he must land like a cat (on hands and knees) in the proper defensive referee's position base. W1 follows up with a forward-moving cat crawl to a switch or stand-up.

Coaching Point

The wrestlers need to know how important it is to quickly crawl out for the switch or stand-up before the opponent has time to adjust.

Setup

W1 is in the standing position with W2 behind and hand locked around W1's waist.

Action

W1 twists around while grasping W2's hands, repositioning them on his outside hip (*a*). At this point, W1 whips his inside arm around W2's shoulder, executing the whizzer and tripping W2's inside leg backward (*b*). W1 finishes the maneuver by pushing W2's head away with his free hand, thus facing W2 for the escape (*c*).

Coaching Point

Emphasize that the whizzer be driven with force to break the offensive wrestler's locked hands around the defensive wrestler's waist. This must immediately be followed by a quick head push away to successfully secure the escape. It is also important not to relax at this point because the offensive wrestler will have the opportunity for a second-effort takedown.

(continued)

Setup

W1 is in the standing position with W2 behind and hands clamped.

Action

In this position, W1 slaps W2's leg on one side, faking a switch, and then executing a switch on the other side (*a-b*).

Coaching Point

A variation of this maneuver is the suicide switch. Again, the defensive wrestler fakes a slap to one side (or both sides) of the offensive wrestler. Then the defensive wrestler drops his head toward the mat. Before the defensive wrestler's head touches the mat, he hits a hard switch. It is a very effective alternative.

Setup

W2 is behind W1 with hands locked in the standing position.

Action

In this position, W1 steps behind one of W2's legs with the arm closest to W2's body around the knee and the other arm controlling W2's opposite wrist (*a*). At this point, W1 falls back and trips W2 as W1 hits a Peterson roll, grasping W2's wrist with both hands (*b*).

Coaching Point

With the standing Peterson roll, the wrestlers must have a firm foundation of proper shoulder position and wrist control before performing this drill.

Maintaining a Good Base

Maintaining a good base is the second essential principle for escapes and reversals. The key is staying in good position, with your head up, buttocks down, knees bent, and elbows in. A good base on the mat in the down position also requires your knees wide, back arched, and elbows at knee width. This principle cannot be overemphasized. I often tell my athletes, "If you get out of good position, the sin is not being there; it's staying there!"

52   BASE-BUILDING DRILL

Setup
After W1 establishes a good base, W2 positions himself on top of W1 in the referee's position.

Action
On the whistle, W2 attempts to break W1 down to the mat as W1 struggles to maintain a good base. W2 should be very physical. The drill should last 15 to 30 seconds.

Coaching Point
Stress to the defensive wrestler the significance of lowering his center of gravity (or hips) when this drill is performed.

53   BELLY-TO-BASE DRILL

Setup
W1 starts on his belly with his elbows in and palms on the mat shoulder-width apart. W2 is sitting or lying on top of W1 with all his weight.

Action
On the whistle, W1 quickly pushes up with both hands to the good base position previously described.

Coaching Point
If the defensive wrestler can perfect this skill, the offensive wrestler will not be afforded the opportunity to shoot a half nelson on one side or the other when the defensive wrestler is on the mat.

Setup

The wrestlers start in the referee's position.

Action

When W2 chops W1's near arm down, W1 dips down only to his elbow. W1 then skates forward with his knee to bring himself back to a good base, pulling with his arms as well.

Coaching Point

Encourage your wrestlers not to be driven to their bellies, which offers opponents the opportunity to take them to their backs.

Setup
The wrestlers start in the referee's position (*a*).

Action
On the whistle, W1 hits a switch, landing on his outside buttock and driving his right hand between W2's legs and spinning (hip-heisting) behind W2 for the reversal (*b*). Next, W2 (becoming W1) performs the switch on the whistle. This continuous (reversing roles) whistle drill lasts 15 to 30 seconds.

Coaching Point
Again, first expose the wrestlers to the Hip-Heist Drill, as illustrated in chapter 6 on pages 219 and 220. Note that inexperienced wrestlers will tend to reach the switch arm over the top wrestler's back. This bad habit must be broken immediately.

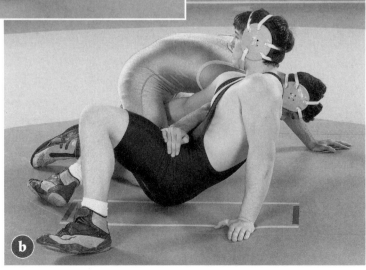

Setup

This is a solitary drill in which each wrestler starts in the defensive referee's position, pretending that the offensive wrestler has mounted him on the left side (*a*).

Action

On the whistle, the wrestler lifts his right knee while simultaneously sitting his left leg in front of him (*b*).

Coaching Point

It is important that the wrestler not let his sit-out leg lag behind because his opponent in a match will have the opportunity to control it and stop the sit-out. The wrestler also must not lean too far back or forward, as is stressed in the following push-and-pull drill.

Setup

After W1 sits out, W2 double-underhooks W1.

Action

At this point, W2 pushes and pulls W1 forward and backward. W1's mission is to scoot forward and backward on his heels, buttocks, and hands in order to keep his upper body perpendicular to the mat.

Coaching Point

This is an outstanding drill for the defensive wrestler to perfect in order to avoid being cradled or snapped back to his shoulders.

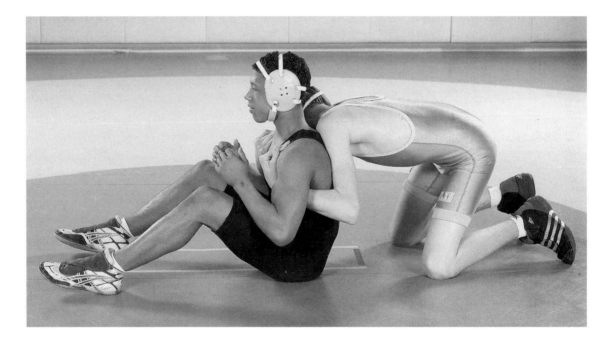

Setup

The wrestlers start in the referee's position.

Action

Granby Roll for a Reversal: In the referee's position, W1 begins by posting his left hand and grabbing W2's wrist with his right hand (*a*). Next, W1 raises his hips (on his toes), making a T with his feet and tucking his chin against his chest. W1 then rolls across the tops of his shoulders, holding W2's wrist and spinning around on top of W2 for the reversal (*b-c*).

(continued)

Granby Roll for an Escape: Performing the same motions for the reversal, W1 rolls across the top of his shoulders, releasing W2's wrist and scoring the escape (*d*).

Coaching Point

Emphasize the coaching point demonstrated in the Upper-Shoulder Roll Drill in chapter 1 on page 22. Remember, your wrestlers must roll on their upper shoulders and no lower.

Escape and Reversal Counter Drills

This section is divided into two general escape and reversal counter areas. Phase one stresses basic counter drills in the lifting and standing positions. In phase two, counter drills on the mat are taught.

Basic Lifting and Standing Drills

Basic lifting and standing drills assist the wrestlers in developing standing-position strategies for taking an opponent to the mat, with or without having hands locked.

59   LIFT AND SWEEP

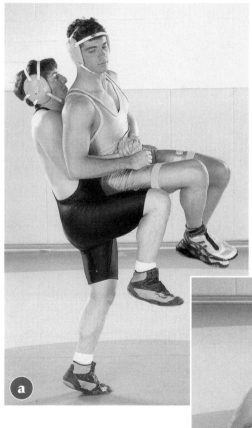

Setup
The wrestlers start in the neutral position with W1 behind W2 with hands locked.

Action
W1 lifts his partner in the air. With one of his knees, W1 sweeps out W2's leg (*a*). Then W1 brings W2 to the mat so that he lands on his side (*b*).

Coaching Point
The offensive wrestler must make sure his knee sweeps at the side of the defensive wrestler's thigh. As always, stress good hip positioning.

Setup

W1 is standing behind W2, who has broken W1's hand lock and is about to escape.

Action

As a last resort, W1 lowers his hip level and leg tackles W2 at knee level or below.

Coaching Point

Lowering the hips and driving into the opponent with the shoulder are important in the successful execution of this drill.

Mat Wrestling Counter Drills

The following drills demonstrate counters that offensive wrestlers can use when down on the mat. They provide the wrestlers with an arsenal of escape-and-reversal restraining maneuvers. Pay particular attention to hip location and the offensive wrestler's center of gravity. Hip position is essential to controlling the defensive wrestler.

61   SWITCH HIGH-LEG COUNTER DRILL

Setup
The wrestlers begin the drill in the referee's position.

Action
On the whistle, W2 switches to one side (*a*). W1 lifts the leg to the side of W2's switch (*b*). W2 switches as high as possible and floats behind W2, who fails to complete the switch. W1 then assumes the referee's position on the other side of W2. W2 hits a switch on the opposite side. This switching from side to side should last 15 to 30 seconds.

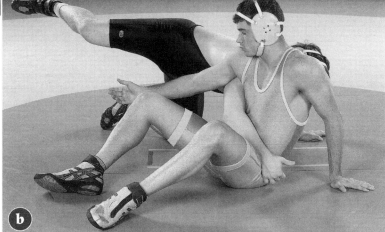

Coaching Point
Stress quick reaction and follow-through by the offensive wrestler when he is lifting his leg and maneuvering behind the defensive wrestler.

Setup

The wrestlers start in the referee's position.

Action

W2 performs a switch. At the same time, W1 limp-arms, whipping the arm out in a circular motion (*a*). W1's palm should face up during the limp-arm reaction. After W1 performs the limp-arm and as W2 falls back, W1 drives his chest to W2's chest while simultaneously shooting a half nelson and crotch (*b*).

Coaching Point

The whipping action of the arm with the palm up is very important when performing this drill. This maneuver is useful when the wrestler knows his opponent usually hits a switch on the whistle.

SIT-OUT SINGLE UNDERHOOK AND CHIN COUNTER DRILL

Setup

The wrestlers start in the referee's position.

Action

When W2 sits out, W1 moves to the side and underhooks W2's near arm. At the same time, W1 chins W2's near shoulder, grabbing W2's chin and forcing W2's back to the mat (*a-b*).

Coaching Point

All action in this drill must be executed simultaneously. The wrestlers must also be taught not to twist the chin to the side when taking an opponent to his back so as to avoid being penalized for unnecessary roughness.

Setup

The wrestlers start in the referee's position.

Action

After W2 sits out, W1 simply drives his chest forward into W2's back and executes a cradle on either side (*a-b*). W1 then drives W2 to his back to complete the drill.

Coaching Point

Be sure that the offensive wrestler drives his chest into the defensive wrestler's back so the defensive wrestler's head is as close as possible to his knees before performing the cradle.

Setup
The wrestlers start in the referee's position.

Action
As W2 begins to execute the Granby roll, W1's right hand locks around W2's upper right arm (*a*). W1 then spins around in the opposite direction of W2's Granby roll, finishing behind W2 (*b-c*).

Coaching Point
Stress the importance of being prepared to counter a Granby roll and lock the arm quickly to follow through by reversing direction. This drill will involve a lot of practice to perfect.

(continued)

GRANBY HEAD-HAND POST ROLL
THROUGH COUNTER DRILL

Setup

The wrestlers start in the referee's position.

Action

When W2 initiates the Granby roll, W1 posts his free hand and head on the mat (*a-b*). W1 then shadows the Granby roll, landing on his knees behind W2 (*c*).

(continued)

Coaching Point

Teach the wrestlers to roll through with their heads, landing on their knees, before working on this Granby roll counter.

Conclusion

The preceding drills lay out the foundation for developing your athletes into solid defensive and offensive wrestlers. Depending on the circumstances you are faced with (scouting reports, minor injuries, and so on), you may need to select those drills appropriate for the situation. Furthermore, you may find it necessary to devise variations of the drills illustrated in this chapter to fit the needs of your wrestlers.

As the year progresses, combine drills to promote flow of motion in the defensive and offensive positions. A vivid example of this strategy is chain wrestling, discussed in chapter 7 on pages 230 and 231.

The skilled wrestler must be prepared to act quickly in the defensive position, demonstrating the ability to change directions. This will keep the offensive wrestler guessing rather than anticipating his opponent's next move. Likewise, the offensive wrestler must be prepared to react to any unexpected maneuver from the defensive wrestler. This can be accomplished only in a wrestling program that stresses proper drill instruction.

In chapter 4 you will direct your attention to riding drills that, when properly performed, can lead to the objective of wrestling—the fall.

Riding to Pinning Combination Drills

Ed Peery

Not doing more than average is what keeps the average down.
William M. Winans

Riding is the ability to control the defensive wrestler while maneuvering for a pinning combination. Controlling the hips is an essential ingredient for riding the defensive wrestler effectively. If the defensive wrestler's hips are not controlled, escapes and reversals are often the result.

When the referee's whistle initiates mat or ground wrestling, the offensive wrestler's goal is to execute breakdowns that control the defensive wrestler's hips. This is accomplished by positioning the defensive wrestler's hips as low as possible.

Wrestling is a position-reflex (or reaction) activity. The wrestler must experience the *feeling* of the offensive position, in addition to learning offensive skills and developing reflexes for various offensive positions. Therefore, realistic resistance by the defensive wrestler is necessary for proper development of riding skills. Insist that the wrestlers take drilling activities very seriously. Drilling, when done effectively, is at least as important as full-contact wrestling, especially in the area of offensive wrestling.

Riding Drills

The offensive wrestler must destroy the defensive wrestler's base and eliminate his motion. To accomplish this goal, the wrestlers must be exposed to a variety of breakdown techniques. The following drills will assist the wrestlers in becoming successful riders.

Setup

The wrestlers start in the referee's position.

Action

W1 stands on his toes and clasps his hands behind his back, then places his chest on W2's upper back (*a*). W1 drives all his weight on W2 from each side, attempting to break W2's body down to the mat (*b*). This drill should last for 30 seconds on each side.

Coaching Point

Emphasize keeping the offensive wrestler's weight and strength on the defensive wrestler. The defensive wrestler must not collapse or drop to his elbows voluntarily. Furthermore, stress that the offensive wrestler should drive down and into the defensive wrestler by using his legs while staying on his feet with knees off the mat. Finally, make sure that the offensive wrestler keeps his hips higher than the defensive wrestler does. This drill is a prerequisite and the foundation for teaching the very important Spin Drill.

Setup
W1 is standing behind W2 with hands locked.

Action
W2 establishes a slightly forward center of gravity. At this point, W1 moves his head to the side of the locked-hands grip on W2's body (*a*). W1 then steps in front of W2's leg on the side of the locked hands and head (*b*). Next, W1 sweeps W2's ankle. Finally, W1 drives into W2 as he sweeps his foot back and up, forcing W2 down to the mat (*c*).

Coaching Point
Ensure that your wrestlers assume a proper rear standing, locked-hands position. This drill takes advantage of the defensive wrestler's center of gravity when he is leaning forward. Although some wrestlers will release the opponent in anticipation of securing a takedown, stress the importance of keeping the opponent under control.

69 TIGHT WAIST-TO-ARM BAR/HALF NELSON DRILL

Setup

The wrestlers start in the referee's position.

Action

W1 applies pressure on W2's near arm while using a tight waist, which drives W2's arm and hips to the mat (*a*). At the conclusion of the breakdown, W1 applies an arm bar (*b*). At this point, W1 jumps to the opposite side, threading the needle for a half nelson (*c*). Turning W2's back to the mat, W1 releases the arm bar to place his arm in W2's crotch (*d*).

Coaching Point

The near-arm and waist breakdown is effective for three reasons. First, it is simple to teach and execute in driving the defensive wrestler off his base. Second, it is not a lot of motion for the offensive wrestler and stresses control, driving the defensive wrestler's hips to the mat. And finally, the movement to a half nelson and crotch-pinning combination is a logical finish to the drill.

Setup

The wrestlers start in the referee's position.

Action

W1 slides the near arm down and grasps W2's wrist while driving his head into W2's armpit (*a*). While driving W2 forward, W1 pulls W2's near wrist backward and lifts it off the mat (*b*). When W2 is flattened on the mat, W1 can work toward the half nelson pinning combination by lifting the head-and-arm lever while forcing his head under W2's arm (*c*). Once W1's head is under W2's arm at the shoulder, great pressure can be exerted on W2's shoulder for turning him over. At this point, the half nelson maneuver can be applied on W2 (*d*).

Coaching Point

The head-and-arm lever breakdown demonstrates basic fundamentals used for destroying the defensive wrestler's base. The result often is an aggressive breakdown leading to an equally dominating pinning combination. The head lever is particularly effective for beginners because it teaches a practical means of using the head as a positive force for breaking the opponent down off his base.

71   FAR-ARM NEAR-ANKLE BREAKDOWN TO HALF NELSON DRILL

Setup

The wrestlers start in the referee's position.

Action

W1 releases W2's near arm and reaches across W2, cupping W2's far arm above the elbow (*a*). At the same time, W1 releases the waist lock to grasp W2's near-leg ankle. W1 accomplishes this by driving his chest into W2 and forcing him off his base to the mat (*b*). W1 then shoots the half nelson and crotch-pin hold on W2. It is important that the half nelson is sunk deep so that W1 has his elbow behind W2's neck (*c*).

Coaching Point

The Far-Arm Near-Ankle Breakdown to Half Nelson Drill demonstrates the mechanics of destroying two opposing points of the defensive wrestler's base and driving him to the mat. Some of your wrestlers may at first feel uncomfortable completely releasing an opponent's arm and waist. Point out that their chest pressure against the defensive wrestler will compensate for the momentary release. In fact, maintaining chest pressure at the whistle is important for the offensive wrestler all the time.

Setup

The wrestlers start in the referee's position.

Action

W1 initiates action by releasing W2's near elbow and driving the inside of the forearm up and across W2's face. At the same time, W1 releases the waist lock and grasps W2's far ankle (*a*). W1 must also drive the crossface to force W2's head toward his outside ankle. W1 moves the hand, grasping the ankle quickly to the back of W2's far knee (*b*). When W2's head is close to his knee, W1 locks hands for the cradle (*c*). W1 then pulls W2 back into a pinning situation (*d*).

Coaching Point

It is important that the offensive wrestler exercise caution while bringing the defensive wrestler to his back. If not, the defensive wrestler can potentially kick through and end up on top in a similar situation. The point of emphasis is that once the offensive wrestler locks hands the position becomes risky. Thus, the offensive wrestler should not rush when forcing the defensive wrestler to his back. Note: This maneuver is recommended for situations in which the pin is essential for team points or getting back into the match.

73 NEAR-ARM/WAIST-TO-CROSSFACE CRADLE DRILL

Setup

The wrestlers start in the referee's position.

Action

W1 breaks W2 down to the mat (*a*). After breaking W2 down, W1 watches for W2's reaction. If W2's head is low or on the mat, it isn't likely that he plans a quick reaction, so W1 can release pressure on the tight waist and near arm. From that point, W1 moves higher and forward in preparation for applying the crossface (*b*). Then, once his legs and feet are positioned, W1 drives the crossface across W2's face, forcing W2's head toward his outside knee (*c*). When the hands are locked, W1 completes the maneuver as previously instructed in the Crossface-Cradle Drill on pages 126 and 127 (*d*). Again, stress caution and deliberation when W1 brings W2 to his back.

Coaching Point

Although the concluding aspect of this drill is the same as the Crossface-Cradle Drill, keep emphasizing proper finishing skills. Never assume anything, including knowledge of drills formerly taught.

Setup
This drill starts with W1 in the back crab-ride position.

Action
First, W1 puts a leg in while blocking W2's elbow on the same side so W2 cannot block as the leg is being applied (*a*). Next, W1 adjusts his position above and across W2's back. W1's outside arm reaches under W2's far arm. He locks hands and forces W2's head down with the inside elbow (*b*). From here, W1 drives W2 to the mat and towad his back (*c*).

Coaching Point
With repetition, most wrestlers will learn this move without difficulty. Both partners should cooperate by resisting the offensive wrestler as he forces the defensive wrestler to the mat. The Crossbody Ride Drill is the first position that should be taught for leg wrestling. The logical progression is to move from the crossbody to the guillotine pinning combination that is discussed next.

Setup

W1 is in the crossbody ride position with W2 on his hands and knees.

Action

Using both arms, W1 secures the trapped arm with inside grips (*a*). W1 raises W2's arm in preparation for forcing the arm overhead (*b*). Once the arm is raised overhead, W1 places the near arm around W2's neck while holding the arm at the wrist (*c*). W1 then lies back into W2's arm, creating pressure that forces

W2's shoulders toward the mat. W1 creates additional pressure by wrapping his arms around W2's head in tandem with arching his back (*d*).

Coaching Point
Emphasize the importance of the offensive wrestler keeping his hips tight and high on the defensive wrestler. Allow the wrestlers to perform this drill many times during practice.

Setup

The wrestlers begin the drill with W1 in the crossbody ride position (*a*).

Action

As W2 sits out with his free leg, W1 overhooks W2's near arm, placing his palm on W2's back (*b*). Simultaneously, W1 hips into W2, driving his shoulder into W2 and lifting his laced leg to the ceiling for further pressure on W2's body (*c*).

Coaching Point

Jacob's Ride is an offspring of the Crossbody Ride Drill in which the defensive wrestler sits out with his free leg. It is very important to stress proper hip and shoulder pressure on the defensive wrestler. If not, the defensive wrestler could react with a short arm-drag for the reversal. The success of this drill depends on much repetition by all your wrestlers. A variation of the Jacob's Ride Drill is the Cross Wrist to Turk Drill, which is illustrated in chapter 5 on pages 171 and 172.

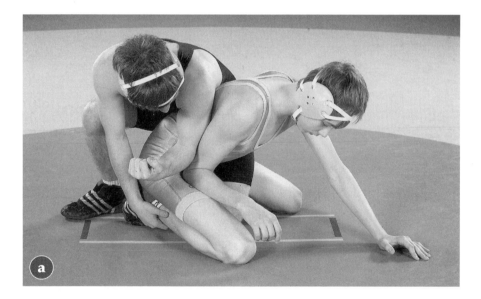

Riding Counter Drills

Wrestling is a sport of action and reaction. The defensive wrestler must be prepared to react without hesitation to the offensive wrestler's ride techniques. This can be accomplished by the defensive wrestler perfecting the following riding counter drills.

77   FREEING HANDS AND WRIST DRILL

Setup
The drill starts with W2 standing behind W1, holding one arm with a two-hand grip on the wrist (*a*).

Action
W1 then maneuvers his free arm under W2's arm, grabbing W2's far hand (*b*). Next, W1 pries up, placing pressure on W2's wrist. This forces W2 to release the near-side grip on W1 (*c*). At this point, W1 extends the arm that W2 still

controls and turns it away from the body, freeing W2's grip on the arm (*d*). Finally, W1 draws his elbows back to the inside position as quickly as possible in preparation for an escape or reversal maneuver.

Coaching Point

While each wrestler takes turns performing this drill, emphasize the importance of the defensive wrestler not reaching across his body, which allows the offensive wrestler to regain wrist control. After standing up, the defensive wrestler must be concerned with keeping his hands and wrists free. There is not much the defensive wrestler can do in the standing position if his hands and wrists are controlled. In essence, the defensive wrestler must free his wrists to free his hands.

Setup

W1 starts in the standing position with his elbows tight against the body and W2 behind him. W2 will also have one arm around the waist and the other hand on W1's biceps. Both wrestlers would have legs bent (*a*).

Action

The drill is initiated by W1 grabbing W2's hand, which is across W1's biceps (*b*). Next, W1 raises his hand while driving his elbow back through W2's armpit (*c*). Finally, W1 backs his hips underneath the lifted arm and finishes in control (*d*).

Coaching Point

This drill is quick because once the defensive wrestler gains control, his drill partner becomes the drill wrestler, performing the same drill. Continue the drill until you want to end it. The goal is for the wrestlers to react to the situation without thinking.

Setup

The starting position for this drill places W1 in the sitting position. W2 has one arm around the waist and the other hand on W1's biceps (*a*).

Action

W1 reaches across his body and grasps W2's wrist, freezing W2's hand on the biceps (*b*). W1 places his head on the mat, performing a turn-in maneuver. At the same time, the arm that W2 controlled raises up and under W2's armpit, reversing W2 (*c*).

Coaching Point

The major advantage of this drill is the development of a reflex action with minimum investment of effort. Like the previous drill, this drill is quick because once the defensive wrestler gains control his drill partner becomes the drill wrestler, performing the same drill. Continue the drill until you want to end it.

80 HALF NELSON BRIDGING COUNTER SOLITARY DRILL

Setup
The wrestlers start this solitary bridge drill by lying on their backs (*a*).

Action
As they bridge on their necks, instruct the wrestlers to touch both ears and roll up, touching their noses to the mat. While in the bridging position, teach the wrestlers to perform upside-down push-ups. Finally, have the wrestlers bridge as high as they can (*b*). In this position, they are to quickly drop down from the bridge, forcing their hips away from an imaginary opponent. At the same time, they are to thrust the fist and arm between the imaginary opponent's chest, recovering to the belly and then to a defensive referee's position base (*c-d*). They should practice forcing their hips to one side and then the other.

Coaching Point

This drill involves bridging, which is not typical in calisthenics. In fact, it is foreign to the majority of other sports, but in wrestling it is a must. Sooner or later all wrestlers are put to their backs. At this point, it is either bridge or get pinned. Many of the younger wrestlers may lack the neck strength for this drill. Allow them to use their hands as props while bridging. Also, you can teach these wrestlers to prop their elbows on the mat to stay off their shoulders. Above all, emphasize to the wrestlers the importance of getting off their backs.

HALF NELSON BRIDGING COUNTER WITH PARTNER DRILL

Setup

This drill is performed the same as the Half Nelson Bridging Counter Solitary Drill (pages 142-143), except now W2 is holding W1 down.

Action

W1 lies on his back and W2 secures a tight half nelson and crotch (*a*). On the whistle, W1 hits a bridge, forcing his outside arm between his and W2's chest (*b*). Next, W1 quickly drops his back to the mat, shooting his outside arm inward while scissoring his inside leg away from W2 (*c*). The drill ends with W1 regaining a defensive referee's position base (*d*). This drill should be repeated while thrusting the outside arm inside with the half nelson and the inside arm outside with the reverse half nelson.

Coaching Point

You should first teach the drill with minimum resistance from the offensive wrestler, gradually building up to full resistance. This drill should be a part of the warm-up exercises in every practice during wrestling season. You can teach many lessons about the sport of wrestling when teaching this drill. First, the team concept is realized by not giving up a fall. Second, the individual concept of being competitive is learned by not quitting when the wrestler is on his back. Finally, the wrestlers learn to give their all and fight to the end.

HALF NELSON COUNTER
FROM THE REFEREE'S POSITION DRILL

Setup

This drill starts in the referee's position.

Action

W2 shoots a half nelson from the knees. W1 quickly locks his arm above the elbow of W2's half nelson arm (*a*). As soon as the arm is hooked, W1 hits a near-side roll (*b*). W1 then springs across W2's chest. Important point: W1 must spring over W2 with chest on chest (*c*). If W1 rolls his back over W2's chest, W2 will just roll through and end up on top again.

Coaching Point

Use this drill during the first days of the wrestling season. Much is learned about wrestling by learning to avoid the pin. It is difficult to stay off your back but much harder to get off your back. Intense drills will assist in eliminating this problem.

Setup

The wrestlers start in the referee's position.

Action

As W2 attempts the head-and-arm lever, W1 drops the near elbow to the mat. At the same time, W1 points the near hand away to prevent W2 from tying up the wrist. Without W2 gaining wrist control, the head-behind-arm maneuver cannot be accomplished.

Coaching Point

This drill emphasizes that the defensive wrestler must avoid letting his wrists, hands, and arms get tied up. The Base-Building Drill (chapter 3, page 98) and the Skating Drill (chapter 3, page 99) are also helpful to achieve this.

This drill and the next demonstrate how to counter the crossbody ride before it is applied.

Setup
The wrestlers start in the referee's position.

Action
The first counter drill to the crossbody ride is the forward knee pinch. Knowing that W2 will attempt the crossbody ride, W1 quickly moves the near knee forward, pinching the far leg.

Coaching Point
As in the cradle, the best defense for the crossbody ride is not allowing the top man to secure it. Furthermore, the scouting report will let the wrestler know in advance that his opponent uses the crossbody ride.

85 ARM BLOCK CROSSBODY RIDE COUNTER DRILL

The second crossbody ride counter drill is the arm block. Not only does this counter block the crossbody ride, but it also affords W1 the opportunity to reverse W2.

Setup
The wrestlers start in the referee's position.

Action
W1 pinches the near arm against his near leg as W2 attempts to apply the crossbody ride (*a*). Next, W1 curls his arm around W2's leg as W2 attempts the crossbody ride (*b*). Finally, W1 pulls W2's leg over his shoulder and head, coming out the back door and securing a reversal (*c-d*).

Coaching Point

Practice partners should repeat these drills many times throughout the season because the crossbody ride is a popular maneuver. By perfecting these two counters, a wrestler not only can stop the crossbody ride but can also eliminate the possibility of the painful guillotine.

Conclusion

Much can be said about riding an opponent. On occasion, I lost the standing (or takedown) phase of the match but dominated the mat or ground phase. Riding control with authority demoralizes the opposing wrestler. Such riding superiority can be accomplished only by drilling.

Drilling is absolutely essential for success in wrestling. You must incorporate drills during every warm-up session. In doing so, make drilling both an active and fun experience. Most important, the coach must be very involved during drilling sessions by directing, observing, and correcting. End every warm-up session with some full-resistance situation wrestling (detailed fully in chapter 7, pages 231-232).

Drilling in the practice room is an imperative activity. Plan it and execute it daily.

Chapter 5 offers more offensive maneuvers for the mat or ground wrestling phase. The initial emphasis of the chapter is on those drills that prepare the wrestlers for pinning combinations, while the latter half covers advanced pinning combinations.

Advanced Pinning Combination Drills

Jim Akerly and Craig Turnbull

*The difference between the impossible and the possible
lies in a person's determination.*
Tommy Lasorda

Wrestling is a sport of positioning. The wrestler who creates and maintains the better hip position is more likely to win. In the offensive position, it's a must. If a wrestler can maintain proper body position while remaining under control, the defensive wrestler will be hard pressed to score an escape or reversal. And this is the prerequisite for working toward the ultimate goal of wrestling: the fall.

The challenge of mat wrestling for the offensive wrestler is to make the defensive wrestler's position longer, driving his hips to the mat. The top wrestler's goal is to destroy his opponent's position and attack for the fall.

Far too often, the offensive wrestler is satisfied with controlling his opponent and fails to finish with a pinning combination. The purpose of the following drills is not only to control the bottom wrestler but to follow up with pinning combinations that secure near-falls or falls.

Chapters 3 and 4 included many drills and counter drills that teach wrestlers how to avoid being pinned. Chapter 4 exposed the reader to a number of related riding-to-pinning drills. The emphasis of this chapter is to introduce more advanced pinning combination drills.

Prepinning Warm-Up Drills

Expose your wrestlers to the following warm-up drills as a prerequisite for demonstrating various pinning situation techniques. Done at the beginning of practice, these warm-up drills not only prepare the wrestlers for the rest of the workout but assist in improving the execution of a number of pinning situations.

Setup

The drill begins with W2 in the referee's position. W1 assumes a chest-to-back position, underhooking W2's arms with the feet hooked above W2's ankles (*a-b*).

Action

On the whistle, W2 rolls and drops to his elbows in many different directions. W2 tries to whip W1 off him while W1 tries to stay against W2's body (*c-d*).

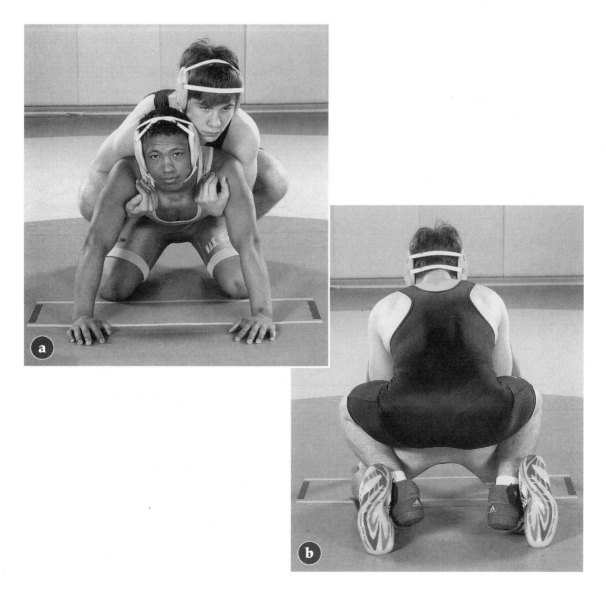

(continued)

Coaching Point

The purpose of this drill is to teach the offensive wrestler to ride the defensive wrestler with tight contact before executing any pinning combination. The drill should last 15 to 30 seconds before partners change positions. Three to five reps per wrestler will suffice.

Setup

W2 is in the referee's position. W1 is on his feet with knees bent, grabbing W2's far hip with both hands (*a*).

Action

W1 tilts W2 by pulling him back into his hips, keeping W2's hips on top of his hips (*b*). Once W2 is pulled back, W1 must attend to pinching his knees against W2's left leg. He must also stay perpendicular to the bottom wrestler (*c-d*).

(continued)

Coaching Point

It is imperative to teach proper tilt positioning. Thus, the offensive wrestler must keep his inside thigh against the defensive wrestler's belly. Each practice partner should take turns performing the Tilt Loading Drill as long as you see fit to do so.

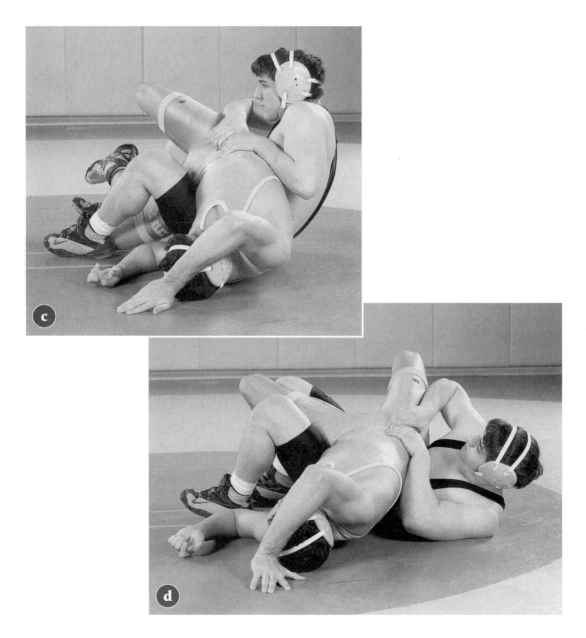

Setup

The wrestlers start in the referee's position.

Action

W1 steps to the side on his toes, wrapping his left arm deep inside W2's far shoulder (*a*). At the same time, W1 keeps his shoulder in W2's armpit, lifting his elbow and forcing W2's arm off the mat (*b*). W1 continues the move by pressuring the far hand and prying the far thigh of W2 in a circular motion (*c*).

(continued)

W1 finishes the drill by securing W2's near wrist, maintaining pressure on W2's back while spinning behind (*d*). From this position, W1 considers his pinning combination options in a match.

Coaching Point

Emphasize that the offensive wrestler should stay off his knees as each partner performs the drill. Remember, drills practiced poorly or without proper technique are a waste of time.

Setup

The wrestlers start in the referee's position.

Action

In this drill, W1 secures W2's near wrist, pulling it inside while pressuring his back (*a*). While constantly exerting pressure on W2's back, W1 places W2's wrist on his back in preparation for a pinning combination (*b-c*).

Coaching Point

The offensive wrestler must stay off the knees when applying pressure to the defensive wrestler's back. Also, should the offensive wrestler have trouble pulling the wrist out, he can reach with his free hand, grabbing the defensive wrestler's four fingers to assist in putting his arm on his back. Finally, the offensive wrestler must not take the arm more than a 90-degree angle to the bottom man's body, or it could become illegal. Observe the drill partners carefully during this drill. Have both wrestlers take turns practicing this drill until you are satisfied they have performed the drill correctly.

(continued)

Advanced Pinning Combination Drills

After the wrestlers have perfected the various breakdown and fundamental fall techniques, you can begin demonstrating higher-level pinning combination drills, such as the following. It is imperative that you devote additional time to demonstrating and observing the wrestlers performing these advanced pinning maneuvers.

90   HIGH HALF NELSON

Setup

W2 is on his chest with W1 scissoring around the near leg. Also, W1 lifts W2's knees off the mat with forward pressure on W2 (*a*).

Action

W1 grabs W2's far wrist with his near hand. Simultaneously, W1 reaches under W2's far arm and grabs his own wrist with his far elbow under W2's far elbow (*b*). W1 then releases the grip he has on his own hand, shooting a deep half nelson. Immediately after applying the half nelson, W1 steps out to the

(continued)

side of the half nelson. W1 should be perpendicular to W2 as he begins to force him to his back (*c*). W1 finishes the drill with his chest on W2's, legs stretched and on his toes, pressing W2's shoulders to the mat for the pin (*d*).

Coaching Point

The offensive wrestler must keep the pressure on by driving off his toes, not his knees. This is another bread-and-butter maneuver that should never be overlooked in the practice room.

Setup

Begin with W2 on his belly with W1 applying a far arm bar and near-side half.

Action

W1 secures an arm bar and applies a half nelson on the opposite side with the hand deep over W2's head (*a*). W1 then pries the half nelson, forcing W2's head away from the arm bar. Loosening the arm bar slightly, W1 begins to turn W2 to his back. W1's hips must be low while on his toes (*b*). The drill is completed with W1 chest to chest against W2, applying a tight half nelson and planting his toes on the mat with his head up (*c*).

Coaching Point

Stress that the offensive wrestler must loosen the arm bar as he deepens the half nelson. The arm bar and half nelson is one of the most successful pinning combinations in wrestling, so wrestlers should practice it often.

(continued)

Setup

The drill starts with W2 on his belly and W1 applying a far half nelson and near arm bar.

Action

W1 tightens the arm bar on the near side and the half nelson on W2's far side (*a*). Next, W1 drives into W2, forcing his arm under on the half nelson side (*b*). W1 drives the side of his back into W2's back, pushing off his feet to complete the arm bar and half stack (*c*).

Coaching Point

The pressure applied by the offensive wrestler pushing off his toes is significant at the conclusion of the drill. Have partners take turns working on this drill until you are satisfied with their performance.

(continued)

Setup

W2 lies on his belly with his left arm in front and slightly bent. W1 has his chest on W2's back while applying an arm bar on W2 (*a*).

Action

W1 reaches his left arm across W2's face and grabs the far pectoral area. W1 then drives W2's far shoulder toward his ear and jams the near knee under W2's near hip, tilting him into a near-fall position (*b*). W1 finishes the drill by hipping into W2 as his right leg reaches across W2's body. W1 also locks his right leg so W2 cannot bridge effectively (*c*).

Coaching Point

The offensive wrestler's hip positioning is very important, so guide the drill partners slowly at first for proper technique. Speed can increase with practice.

(continued)

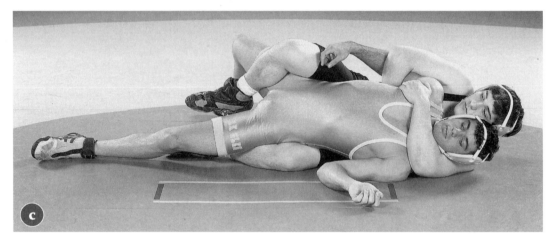

Setup

The wrestlers start in the referee's position with W1 in a basic two-on-one arm ride on W2's left arm.

Action

W1 drives W2's belly to the mat, executing a crossface with his left arm while still controlling W2's left wrist with his right hand (*a*). Next, W1 quickly releases W2's wrist just prior to reaching for W2's near leg (*b*). At the same time, W1 keeps body pressure on W2 by driving off his feet into W2. Continuing the drill, W1 picks up W2's near leg at the knee with his right hand while wrapping his right leg around W2's far leg (*c*). W1 finishes the maneuver by driving

(continued)

across W2, placing him on his back. He also lifts W2's head off the mat with his left hand and posts his right hand on the mat to maintain balance when completing the Turk Ride (*d*).

Coaching Point

Make sure that the offensive wrestler drives off his feet to keep the pressure on the defensive wrestler prior to lifting the defensive wrestler's near leg. The wrestlers will have to spend some time perfecting this drill under the supervision of the coaches. This drill will likely take more time to perfect.

Setup

The wrestlers start in the referee's position.

Action

W1 secures W2's near wrist with his left hand while placing his left thigh under W2's belly. At the same time, W1 puts his right thigh against W2's near-side buttock (*a*). W1 then drives W2 to his near shoulder, staying tightly against him. Also, W1 reaches across W2's belly, grabbing W2's left wrist with his right hand. While in this two-on-one position, W1 pulls W2 to his back (*b*). W1 completes the drill with his body perpendicular to W2 and under W2's body. W1 also pinches W2's thigh with his knees, keeping his feet close to his buttocks (*c*). To avoid a defensive fall, W1 must constantly be aware of his shoulder position.

Coaching Point

Hand control and proper positioning of the hips are important. Likewise, the offensive wrestler must be careful not to place his shoulders on the mat, or a defensive fall could occur. Proper technique is an important factor when performing this pinning combination drill, so observe the wrestlers carefully. Do not permit a wrestler to perform this move in competition until he has perfected it to your satisfaction.

(continued)

Conclusion

The main objective for every wrestler should be to score a pin or fall. However, sometimes pinning combination skills are not developed thoroughly in the mat sport. Too many wrestlers devote less time drilling in the offensive position than they devote to takedown skills. Thus, it is the responsibility of the coach to devote the appropriate amount of practice time to pinning combinations.

From a developmental perspective, creating the attitude and skills associated with scoring from the top position early in a wrestler's training will increase his ability to control his opponent and score pins. Strong skills from the offensive position will not only physically wear down the wrestler's opponent but will ultimately lead to more pins during a wrestler's career. In successful wrestling programs, winners are also pinners.

Conditioning is another important aspect of successful wrestling. Any wrestler can perfect moves through drill work, but if he is not well conditioned failure on the mat is a distinct possibility. Chapter 6 introduces effective conditioning drills. Coaches need to place as much emphasis on conditioning as they do on wrestling skill development. After all, how often have you seen skilled wrestlers defeated by less-skilled opponents who were in better shape? The conditioning drills offered in chapter 6 will prepare wrestlers for the physical and mental aspects of the sport, which are essential for experiencing lasting success on the mats.

Conditioning Drills

Ken L. Taylor

There are no secrets to success. It is the result of preparation,
hard work, and learning from failure.
General Colin L. Powell

The purpose of conditioning skills is to supplement (not replace) wrestling. All conditioning drills should be developed with the objective of having maximum carryover to the sport itself. This is called *specificity of exercise*. Your goal is to make each conditioning drill as specific to wrestling as possible.

Fortunately, this is not difficult because wrestling requires so many different levels of fitness: strength, quickness, agility, endurance, flexibility, balance, and mental toughness. Wrestling is considered by many to be the most strenuous and physically demanding sport of all. So, just about any conditioning drill will have benefits for the wrestlers.

The use of conditioning drills for wrestling can accomplish the following objectives:

- **Improved strength.** Conditioning is used to increase strength in the off-season and maintain strength during the season.
- **Increased agility and quickness.** Developing these skills helps the wrestler to control his body in different positions and to be quicker on his feet and on the mat.
- **Enhanced endurance.** Wrestlers with developed cardiovascular endurance are able to finish strong in matches, recover more quickly, and handle the rigors of a strenuous season.
- **Training variety.** Conditioning drills are just different enough from technique drills to alleviate tedium and keep wrestlers interested in practice.
- **Mental benefits.** Good conditioning promotes mental toughness and improves confidence.

Strength Drills

The four major benefits of an effective strength program for wrestling are as follows:

1. A strength program should make wrestlers better, so it's best to concentrate on exercises that use the wrestling muscles.
2. A stronger athlete is less prone to injury and will recover from injury more quickly.
3. A stronger, well-conditioned athlete can hold up to the rigors of a tough season.
4. A stronger wrestler is a more confident wrestler. He feels more able to compete and doesn't feel the misguided need to cut an inordinate amount of weight.

The first and most important goal of strength development for wrestling is *core strength*. The *core* refers to the stabilizing muscles in the center of the body, which include the hips, torso, and lower back. If you think of the body as a series of electrical pathways, you must have a good electrical conductor to carry the current. Think of your midsection as a sponge. Without a conductor ("water"), the electrical current will not travel. The water represents a well-developed core. The stronger the core, the more efficiently energy can be transferred without being lost in the sponge.

Second, wrestling necessitates a lot of driving with the legs and pulling with the arms, so strength conditioning should address those actions.

Third, wrestling is one of the few sports where neck strength is very, very important.

Fourth, wrestlers need endurance strength to remain strong throughout the entire match, especially if a tie occurs and further wrestling is required.

Finally, lifting should integrate different muscle groups at the same time. Wrestling takes place on a three-dimensional plane: up and down, left and right, forward and backward. So strength training should involve movement in all directions.

In the exercises that follow, you will see many balancing exercises as well as lifting that involves movement from one plane to another. These exercises are designed to bring many different muscles into play at the same time. This not only promotes strength in isolated muscles but also increases in balance, flexibility, speed, and agility.

We want to create more powerful wrestlers. By definition, power is the product of force and speed. Power is definitely one thing we hope to gain in a good strength and conditioning program.

It is generally believed that strength gains are better accomplished through heavier weight and fewer reps (several sets of 4 to 8 reps), whereas muscular endurance is achieved with a combination of lower weight and higher reps (sets of 10 to 15 reps or more). I am not a big fan of high-weight, low-rep lifting unless athletes are properly taught, supervised, and spotted. With heavy lifting, the potential for serious injury increases, as does the tendency for athletes to "cheat" or use improper form. The last thing any wrestling coach wants is for one of his wrestlers to be injured in the weight room, especially during the season. In-season lifting should focus on endurance lifting, except for a select few wrestlers who are trying to gain weight.

In-Season Lifting Program

There is a place for lifting during the wrestling season. However, one should not lift just for the sake of lifting. Lifting activities must be organized in such a manner that the muscle groups worked are those used in wrestling. If not, the lifting program will be ineffective.

Big 10

The Big 10 is a group of buddy-lifting exercises we do once a week during the season at the conclusion of practice. These exercises help with strength and endurance and enhance all the major muscle groups used in wrestling.

Keep these guidelines in mind when doing these lifting exercises:

1. Each wrestler needs a buddy who is about the same weight. Heavyweights may need to lift a lighter person (coach or extra person).
2. Do one lift at a time with each partner, alternating and keeping the team together.
3. As the wrestlers get in better shape during the season, gradually increase the reps and distances involved.

The Big 10 approach is a very effective use of practice time. Following is a list of the 10 exercises that make up the Big 10:

1. Piggyback Carry. One partner carries the other piggyback style around the mat once or twice. Switch partners for each carry. This activity develops leg, arm, and back strength.

2. Belly-to-Back Carry. With the belly-to-back carry, the partners go only about one-half the distance as the piggyback carry. This exercise assists the participants in proper lifting techniques and strengthens the back muscles.

3. Buddy-on-Back Squats. One partner is in the piggyback position as the drill partner squats for 10 to 15 reps while facing close to the wall. Emphasize deep squats. This conditioning drill strengthens the legs.

4. Reverse Body Lifts. The drill partner in the standing position initiates the drill by facing opposite his partner with arms around the back of the body and hands locked in front (*a*). At this point, the drill partner would lift his partner off his feet from side to side (*b*). The reverse body lifts would conclude after 8 to 10 lifts for each drill partner (*c*). This drill develops arm, chest, and back strength and proper lifting skills.

5. Handstand Push-Ups. The drill partner does push-ups while his partner holds his feet in the air, standing behind (*a-b*). Each partner should perform 8 to 10 reps. This conditioning activity develops arm and chest strength in various body positions.

6. Pull-Ups. The drill partner is laying on his back with his partner standing and straddling him while each partner grasps the other's wrists (*a*). The drill partner then pulls himself up (*b*). Each practice partner executes 15 to 20 reps. This drill increases grip strength as well as arm and pectoral strength.

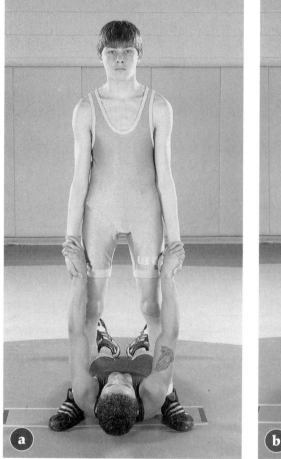

7. Head-Between-Legs Lift. The drill partner is on all fours with his head between his partner's legs. His partner is lying over the drill partner's back (*a*). The drill partner then lifts his partner off the mat (*b*). Each partner performs 6 to 10 reps. This drill strengthens the back muscles for lifting.

8. Four-Way Neck Exercises. The drill partner is on all fours with his partner behind him. The partner then forces the drill partner's neck in different directions: down (*a*), up (*b*), and from side to side (*c*). The drill partner should give moderate neck resistance. Both partners perform six to eight reps in each direction.

9. Abdominal Drill. The standing partner throws the drilling partner's legs toward the mat, straight down to the left and right (*a-b*). Each wrestler should do 20 to 30 reps. This activity develops the abdominal muscles as the drilling partner brings his legs back up.

10. Fingertip Push-Ups. Have your athletes do 40 to 80 reps of push-ups on their fingertips. Push-ups develop the arm and chest muscles.

Weight-Room Lifting

Do a weightlifting circuit with very little rest (10 to 15 seconds) between each lift, lifting for 20 to 30 seconds. If you use partners, one must immediately follow his partner then rush to the next station. This program can be performed two days a week.

The alternate-day program is designed for three sets of six reps, but consider starting with just one or two sets so the wrestlers won't be too sore. Using eight stations, the partners should rotate from station to station. (Note: When using free weights, it's up to you to determine the appropriate poundage for each wrestler.)

Day 1

- **Station 1: Front Squat.** The wrestler holds the barbell in front, resting on his shoulders, and does full squats, developing leg and back strength.

- **Station 2: Standing Cable Pull.** The wrestler does one set of 10 reps with each leg forward to simulate a single-leg pull-in, increasing grip and arm strength. Legs should be slightly bent.

- **Station 3: Pillar Bridge Front.** The wrestler is on his knees and elbows. He raises the right arm and left leg and then the left arm and right leg. This drill strengthens the hips and buttocks.

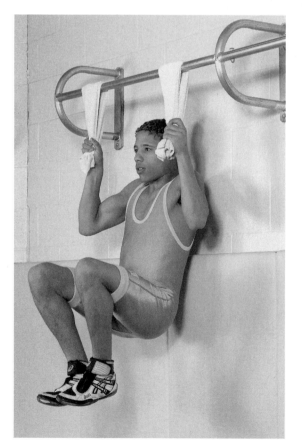

- **Station 4: Towel Pull-Up.** The wrestler wraps two towels around the pull-up bar before performing the pull-up activity. This promotes grip, arm, and chest strength.

- **Station 5: Four-Way Neck Exercise.** Follow the same procedures as for the four-way neck exercises listed on page 186. Note: The number of repetitions would be the same.

- **Station 6: Upper-Body Twist.** The wrestler moves from side to side on a physioball with a free weight. This activity promotes flexibility and strength in the back muscles, as well as improved arm and grip strength.

- **Station 7: Abdominal Crunch.** With a free weight, the wrestler straightens and bends his hips backward and forward (similar to a sit-up) on the physioball. This exercise increases grip, arm, and abdominal strength.

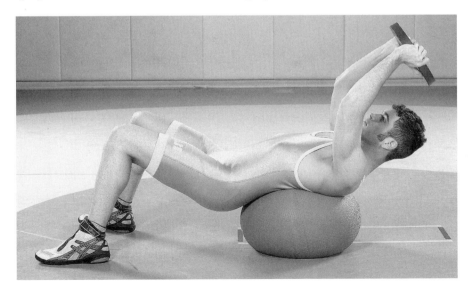

- **Station 8: Leg Curl.** This exercise is performed on the leg machine, straightening (*a*) and bending (*b*) at the knees. This strengthens the hamstrings, calves, and thighs.

Day 2

- **Station 1: Dumbbell Single-Leg Squat.** The wrestler holds dumbbells with one foot on the bench and the other on the floor, dipping and raising his body. This improves leg strength and flexibility.

- **Station 2: Dumbbell Single-Leg RDL.** Holding dumbbells, the wrestler bends forward, lifting the left leg, then returns to the upright position. He then repeats the exercise with the right leg. This strengthens the hip muscles and promotes flexibility and grip strength.

- **Station 3: Dumbbell Alternating Arm Press.** Using the incline bench in the sitting position, the wrestler lifts the right dumbbell to the ceiling and brings it back down to the starting position, then repeats the exercise with the left arm. This activity, like push-ups, strengthens the triceps and chest muscles.

- **Station 4: Physioball Push-Up.** The wrestler does push-ups with hands and feet on physioballs. This is not only a strength drill but also promotes body balance.

- **Station 5: Reverse Hyperextensions.** Using the physioball, the wrestler lies with his belly on the ball and then lifts his legs as high as he can, posting his hands. This drill is effective for hip strength and flexibility.

- **Station 6: High Pull.** Standing with a barbell held at knee level (*a*), the wrestler lifts the barbell to his chest (*b*). This activity strengthens the back and arms.

- **Station 7: Back Hyperextensions.** Lying on his belly on a bench and holding a weight (*a*), the wrestler bends his torso down and back up (*b*). This strengthens the back.

- **Station 8: Dumbbell Alternating Arm Curls.** Performing hammer curls, the wrestler lifts one arm at a time. Make sure palms are facing in. This weightlifting exercise increases biceps strength.

As midseason approaches, "mat time" is at a premium, so you may want to use high-intensity weight circuit training only once a week. You can effectively do this by combining lifts from day 1 and day 2 into a single circuit.

If you really want to get your athletes' heart rates up and keep them up, have only one wrestler at each station, letting them rest only during the 10- to 15-second interval between each station.

With a large number of stations, a good idea is to alternate your stations into upper-body lifts and lower-body lifts as the wrestlers move from station to station. This promotes overall body strength and conditioning without overtaxing one part of the body. You don't want your wrestlers so exhausted during the circuit that they have to quit on their lifts. Also, with your help, the wrestlers should use the proper amount of weight to be able to really push themselves, but not so much that they cannot complete the lifts.

I encourage my wrestlers not to rest while lifting. If they must rest, they should "catch their breath" while their bodies are still being stressed. For example, if they are doing pull-ups, they should rest while still hanging from the bar, and not quit by dropping to the floor. Rest while lifting weights should occur when the weight is in the air, not on the ground!

Off-Season Lifting Program

During the off-season, each of the in-season lifts can be performed with additional lifts added as needed. Off-season lifting can take place three or four days a week. Wrestlers may lift three or four sets, increase the weight appropriately, and dramatically increase the time spent lifting.

The following are additional lifts and exercises, which can also be a part of any weight-training program during the wrestling season:

   1. **Hang Clean.** The wrestler brings the barbell from his hips to his shoulders with palms facing his body (*a-b*). This activity strengthens the arms, legs, and back.

    2. Power Clean. The hang clean and power clean are two of my favorite lifts. It is usually better to teach the athletes how to hang clean first. The wrestler finishes the power clean the same as the hang clean, except the lift is started from the floor. This strengthening exercise is also beneficial for the legs, arms, and back.

    3. Flat Bench Press. You can use either a straight bar or dumbbells, lifting both arms at the same time or alternating arm presses. This exercise also assists in developing the triceps.

4. Good Morning Squat–Jerk Complex. This is a series of athletic lifts performed in succession from the standing position. The barbell is initially on the shoulders with the body bent forward and legs straight (*a*). At this point, the wrestler squats and jerks the barbells over his head (*b-c*). These exercises strengthen the back, arms, and legs.

5. Wide-Hand Snatch. This exercise is executed in a single motion, lifting the barbell from the floor to overhead. The knees are initially bent (*a*). When lifting, the wrestler shifts his body under the barbell (*b*). The exercise finishes with legs and arms straight, with the barbell over the head (*c*). This activity is beneficial for strengthening the arm, leg, and back muscles.

6. Dumbbell One-Arm Snatch. This exercise is executed in a single motion, with the wrestler lifting one dumbbell with one hand from the floor to over his head (*a-b*). The wrestler alternates the lifting arm on each repetition during this activity. This exercise develops the legs, arms, and back.

7. Rope Climbing. This is one of my favorite exercises for wrestling, especially using arms only. There is no better activity for arm and grip strength. Always have "spotters" during this activity as a safety precaution.

8. Lunge Across the Mat. This is another outstanding strength exercise for wrestling. It can be done by holding dumbbells at one's sides or by holding them on the shoulders (*a*). It is important that the wrestler take a deep stride on each step, lifting his knee high (*b*). This drill develops arm, leg, and back strength.

9. Pull-In From Push-Up Position. In the push-up position, the wrestler lifts the dumbbell toward his shoulder with one arm. The wrestler commonly alternates arms after 10 reps. This activity increases arm strength and improves balance.

10. Chin-Up Bar Pull-In. The wrestler holds the chin-up bar with hands together, with palms facing opposite directions. He then attempts to lift his belly up to the bar. Use a spotter. This exercise promotes grip, arm, and abdominal strength.

Cardiovascular Drills

Except for wrestling, there is no substitute for running to develop cardiovascular fitness or efficiency. Wrestlers gain many benefits from running, such as the following:

1. Running promotes cardiovascular endurance.
2. Running increases strength in the legs and hips, especially hill running.
3. Running burns more calories in less time than just about any other activity.
4. Running is an outstanding off-season activity. It would be wise to encourage your wrestlers to compete in cross-country and other running-oriented sports.
5. Running is a great way to get some sunshine and fresh air.

We strongly encourage our wrestlers to run on Sundays and on their days off. This helps to eliminate soreness in the body and rejuvenates one's energy level. The distance can vary from two to four miles or more—whatever is comfortable for each individual wrestler. We believe that Sunday runs lead to better results during the week.

Running and Related Activities During Practice

We have the wrestlers run at different times throughout practice. Note, wrestlers can wear wrestling shoes when running on the mat but should wear running shoes everywhere else. The following are ideas for practice running and related activities:

1. Before stretching at the beginning of practice, the wrestlers can run for 5 to 10 minutes, starting slow and gradually picking up the pace. Related running activities include skipping, high-knee running, sideways running, and leap running. Be creative and make it fun.

2. The wrestlers can run between teaching sessions or in preparation for live wrestling during practice.

3. Interval training, a jogging and sprinting activity, should be introduced midseason. Wrestling is a sport of both endurance and interval activity. Interval running helps your wrestlers adapt to this kind of action. A rule of thumb for interval training is to sprint for 30 seconds and for rest 30 seconds. The duration of interval training should be 6 to 12 minutes.

4. Stair running is great for leg strength because it is more strenuous than traditional running.

5. The stationary bike is a great alternative to running. It is especially effective for wrestlers with knee or ankle problems. But note that wrestlers will have to work twice as long on stationary bikes to work off the same amount of calories as running.

Cardiovascular Drills for Concluding Practice

At the end of practice, the following activities can be used.

Rope Skipping

This is a fantastic activity for promoting quickness and lightness on the wrestler's feet. It assists with balance and coordination and can be an excellent workout in itself. I highly recommend wrestler Buddy Lee's books and videos on rope skipping. Buddy is an unbelievable performer and rope skipper, and his ropes are ultra fast. See www.buddyleejumpropes.com.

LOBO Round-Up

Another unique and creative activity for the conclusion of practice is the "LOBO round-up." We perform the LOBO round-up every so often as a motivating, change-of-pace activity. The wrestlers really like it. Here are the particulars of the drill:

1. Turn on the music nice and loud. Coaches, choose the music or your wrestlers will play something you hate!

2. The wrestlers work in pairs with partners of approximately the same weight.

3. Divide the wrestlers as evenly as possible into six groups for station drills.

4. Get 10-pound plates from the weight room for station 3. The number of plates needed is one-sixth the number of wrestlers.

5. Place each group at one of the six stations.

6. On the whistle, the wrestlers begin the activity at their station. The drill at each station should last 20 to 30 seconds. At each station, each partner does two alternating intervals. On the coach's whistle, the groups move to the next station. The interval of time to move to the next station should be no longer than 15 seconds before starting the next activity. The stations are as follows:

   • **Station 1:** Partner A sprints across the room and back while partner B rests. Then partner B sprints while partner A rests. (Remember, the partners in each group do two intervals at each station.)

- **Station 2:** Partner A does the designated number of push-ups with his legs propped on partner B's back, then the partners reverse roles.

- **Station 3:** Partner A lunges forward while holding the 10-pound weight in front of him, keeping arms extended. He alternates between the left leg stepping forward and the right leg stepping forward (*a*). At the same time, partner B does squats while holding the 10-pound plate over his head, arms always extended. He must do full squats, so the thighs come down parallel to the floor (*b*). The partners then switch 10-pound plate drills.

• **Station 4:** Partner A does the designated number of abdominal crunches while partner B holds his legs down on the mat. They then reverse positions.

• **Station 5:** Partner A performs "ski" jumps across partner B's back. At this station, one partner is on his elbows and knees while the other stands beside him, facing the same direction and alternately jumping from side to side. They then rotate positions.

- **Station 6:** Partner A jumps vertically as many times as he can during the time frame determined by the coach. He must jump as high as he can, lifting his knees as high as possible (*a*). At the same time, partner B performs a "wall sit" with his back against the wall and upper thighs parallel to the floor (*b*). He stays in that position as long as partner A vertically jumps. They then change positions.

Agility and Quickness Drills

Position, technique, agility, and quickness are vital in wrestling. We must teach our wrestlers to set up their moves by creating motion, maneuvering the opponent out of position, and striking when the opponent is off balance or out of sync.

Even countermoves are best executed by the wrestler positioning himself in a way that stymies his opposition, taking advantage of his weaknesses and ultimately scoring.

The following activities will assist the wrestlers in developing instincts that will promote good timing and body positioning, proper motion, and agility and quickness.

SHADOW WRESTLING
FROM THE NEUTRAL POSITION

At the beginning of practice, shadow wrestling is a solitary activity that allows each wrestler to focus on motion, body position, and timing. We use shadow wrestling at the end of practice to work on endurance. Start very slowly and gradually increase speed. Make sure every part of the wrestlers' bodies are where they should be.

Setup
Shadow wrestling is initiated from the neutral position.

Action
The participants shadow wrestle various takedowns, increasing speed as they loosen up. This is a great way to work on defense: proper body position, protecting legs, and reacting. It should be composed of three to four periods of 30 seconds, doing as many moves as possible to promote endurance.

Coaching Point
Shadow wrestling improves quickness because it takes away an opponent's resistance, allowing the wrestler to move freely. Emphasize this during the drill. Make sure the wrestlers focus on stance, level change (hip positioning), penetration, and finishes.

SHADOW WRESTLING
FROM THE BOTTOM REFEREE'S POSITION

Setup

Shadow wrestling that initiates from the bottom referee's position.

Action

The wrestlers should concentrate on creating motion, getting the hips moving correctly, and exploding off the bottom. The wrestlers usually perform three to four periods of 30 seconds, doing as many moves as possible.

Coaching Point

This is an excellent coaching tactic to work on all bottom maneuvers: stand-ups, switches, sit-out series, Granby rolls, hip heists, and so on. At the conclusion of practice, stress shadow wrestling off the bottom to work on quickness and endurance.

Setup

The partners start in the neutral position.

Action

Each wrestler reaches in and tries to slap his partner's knees, focusing on slapping the lead knee. Each wrestler is awarded a point when he slaps his partner's knee hard.

Coaching Point

Stress that the wrestlers be light on their feet, quickly moving backward when their partners attempt to slap.

Setup

In the neutral position, each wrestler locks his hands behind his back.

Action

On the whistle, the partners try to step on each other's feet, keeping track of who scores the most points.

Coaching Point

Stress the importance of quickness when performing this drill.

Setup

The coach can invent all kinds of agility and quickness drills by putting the wrestlers in different situations.

Action

In practice, make up a wrestling situation for the athletes to act out then blow the whistle. Following are three ideas for such agility and quickness situation drills.

The Quick Stand

Have the wrestlers lie on their backs, side by side, in opposite directions. On the whistle, the wrestlers quickly come to the standing position. The partner who gets to his feet first scores a point.

(continued)

The Leg Break Away

Have each wrestler hold one of his partner's legs, facing the partner. On the whistle, the wrestlers attempt to break away from each other. The partner who breaks away first scores the point.

The Double-Cradle Fight

Have the partners cradle each other. On the whistle, the wrestler who wins the cradle battle scores.

Coaching Point

Allow the wrestlers to compete full speed for a few seconds. During this time, emphasize the importance of quickness, agility, balance, and proper technique when wrestling maneuvers are performed.

Setup
Wrestlers stand in lines facing the coach.

Action
When the coach points to the left, the wrestlers throw the right leg back. Next, when the coach motions to the right, the wrestlers throw the left leg back. When the coach points to himself, the wrestlers change levels and penetrate toward the coach. And finally, when the coach points to the wrestlers, they scoot backward.

Coaching Point
Stress quickness and proper technique when performing the penetration part of the drill.

Setup

With one partner on all fours, the top partner puts his chest on the bottom man's back.

Action

On the whistle, the top man spins in one direction, changing direction when the coach blows the whistle. This drill should last approximately 30 seconds for each partner.

Coaching Point

Encourage the top man to stay off his knees while moving left or right.

Setup

In this solitary drill, the wrestler starts on his toes and hands with belly up (*a*).

Action

Each wrestler does a series of hip heists on the mat, hip-heisting one direction and then the other (*b-c*). Or, the wrestler does a series of moves that involve starting from the feet. He takes a penetration step, then sprawls, and finally performs a hip heist.

Coaching Point

When performing this drill, the wrestler's legs must hip-heist under each other, never over each other.

(continued)

Wrestling Endurance Drills

Becoming a champion is like wrestling a gorilla. You don't stop when you get tired—you stop when the gorilla gets tired.

I think that endurance for wrestling comes primarily from wrestling. One can build up a lot of endurance by hard drilling of wrestling moves and a lot of live wrestling. If a wrestler stays active during most of his daily practices, he will naturally get into shape.

I believe in alternating hard workouts with moderate, less strenuous workouts so that the wrestlers have a chance to recover and rebuild. Endurance drills can be varied in level of difficulty and length, depending on how hard you want to push your wrestlers.

The following are endurance (or toughness) drills that you can choose for your practice sessions.

Shadow Wrestling   The wrestlers should perform this drill (see pages 211-212 for descriptions and photos) at the end of practice for endurance. It should last 30 seconds or more and be repeated up to three times in the neutral position and then on the bottom position.

Chain Wrestling   Although this is an outstanding activity for promoting technique, it can also be used as a drill to increase endurance. I like this drill because it helps wrestlers avoid mental breakdowns (losing concentration, forgetting to continue movement by acting and reacting, and so on).

This drill should last anywhere from 30 seconds up to two minutes. Chain wrestling is discussed in greater depth in chapter 7 (pages 230-231).

Black Flag Day   This activity allows wrestlers to devote an entire practice to "doing their own thing." The wrestlers are required to work out continuously for approximately an hour, performing any physical wrestling-oriented activity of their choosing. Not only is this a great way to promote overall conditioning, but it allows the wrestlers the freedom to do what they want the entire practice, as long as they keep moving. They can do skill drilling as long as they wish and/or wrestle competitively until the end of practice. This activity is great for varying practice late in the season. The change of pace helps in eliminating staleness. It is a hard practice, but the tough wrestlers really like it.

Setup

The participants start in a neutral tie-up position.

Action

The drill includes full-contact tie-ups, pushing and shoving your partner for 20 to 30 seconds. A variation involves the wrestlers trying to drive each other out of the circle. The wrestler who forces his opponent out of the circle or snaps him down to his hand(s) or knee(s) receives a point.

Coaching Point

This drill encourages mental and physical toughness and aggressiveness. Emphasize that the wrestlers should be very physical, almost to the point of fighting. Of course, you must monitor this drill carefully.

Setup

The wrestlers start in the overhook and underhook neutral position, chest to chest.

Action

On the whistle, each partner works for underhooks while pushing into the other partner. This aggressive activity should last 30 seconds or more and be repeated by each partner up to three times.

Coaching Point

Do not allow the wrestlers to attempt throws or takedowns; just pummeling should occur. This drill is a great way to keep the sweat going. Use this drill as a warm-up activity, starting slowly and gradually becoming more intense. It is a good way to warm up the chest, arms, and shoulders. The activity is also appropriate at the end of practice.

Conclusion

After a lively practice workout filled with vigorous conditioning drills, a cool-down period is mandatory. We finish our more strenuous practices by having the wrestlers walk around the mat room several times to cool down.

I also believe that "draining the legs" is important. We have each wrestler lie on his back with his buttocks against the wall and his feet as high as possible against the wall. It is my belief that this "resting" position promotes blood flow back to the heart and fresh legs for the next day.

It is also a great idea for wrestlers to do some additional stretching, receive additional wrestling instruction, or get a pep talk from the coaches. Humor is also a great way to conclude practice, along with an orange or popsicle treat.

Chapter 7 offers the coach sound practice formats in which drills are an integral facet of the workout session. It also outlines an off-season agenda for developing a successful wrestling program that every coach must promote.

Effective Practices and Off-Season Activities

Bill Welker

Perseverance is a great element of success.
If you only knock long enough and loud enough
at the gate, you are sure to wake up somebody.

Henry Wadsworth Longfellow

The success of your scholastic wrestling program will depend largely on how well you prepare practice sessions from day to day. It is important to realize that your daily practices must evolve with the needs of the athletes participating in the program. For example, if you are working with young and inexperienced wrestlers, you will need to spend more time on the perfection of fundamental techniques. After that, you can begin to move on to more advanced wrestling skills.

Preseason Daily Practice Sessions

Many state high school associations designate dates when participating schools may begin organized wrestling practices. Because a six-week training period is considered ideal in preparing wrestlers for competitive action, it would be to your advantage to schedule wrestling dual meets and tournaments with at least this amount of preseason practice time.

Preseason practices should start with conditioning activities and passive to semiactive drill work. In the first two weeks of practice, emphasis should be on preparing the wrestlers for wrestling.

Following are some examples of conditioning drills for strength, quickness, agility, endurance, flexibility, balance, and mental toughness that can be implemented during preseason practices:

- **Strength:** Big 10, weight-room lifting, and rope climbing (chapter 6).
- **Quickness, agility, flexibility, and balance:** Spin Drill (chapter 1), stretching exercises, shadow wrestling (on feet and bottom), quickness and agility games, hip heist, and rope skipping (chapter 6).
- **Endurance and mental toughness:** stair running, Ironman Drill, and LOBO round-up (chapter 6).

Always remember, if you begin active wrestling before the participants are properly conditioned, you may find yourself facing an abundance of injury problems. Moreover, when you do begin all-out wrestling in practice, it would be wise to start with mat (or ground) wrestling first and gradually work into active takedown wrestling.

This is also the time of year you will want to iron out your wrestlers' fundamental skills, discuss new rule changes and review healthy weight-management practices. Keeping with this philosophy at the beginning of the year will make for a safer and more rewarding season.

In-Season Daily Practice Sessions

The last two weeks of preseason practice should resemble your in-season practice sessions. At this point in the year, it is suggested that you don't teach any new moves, but stress the perfection of previously taught maneuvers via drills and active wrestling.

The wrestling workout session is the most important phase of practice for two reasons. First, it allows you the opportunity to observe the wrestlers more thoroughly and correct their weak areas. Second, it is the best conditioning activity for preparing your wrestlers for competitive action.

On days before dual meets or tournaments, practice should be very light so the wrestlers get sufficient rest for their matches. A few conditioning exercises and wrestling drills would be adequate. If the dual meet or tournament begins early the next day, a discussion period and pep talk would suffice.

Of course, those wrestlers with weight-management problems may have to do additional work. This would include endurance and cardiovascular activities, such as rope skipping, interval running, or riding the stationary bike to make weight (detailed in chapter 6). However, they should be close to match weight the day before competition. This time should be spent thinking about their opponents and wrestling, not thinking about food and making weight. If a wrestler is constantly dwelling on weight problems, you must step in and sternly suggest that he move up a weight class for his own physical and psychological well-being.

At the start of practice following a dual meet or tournament, point out mistakes made by individual wrestlers. They may need to work on their bridging skills, in which case you would reteach the Half Nelson Bridging Counter With Partner Drill (see chapter 4, pages 144-145). Or if they had trouble countering the double-leg takedown, you might revisit the Double-Leg Reaction Counter Drill (see chapter 2, pages 74-75).

On the flip side, don't forget to praise those team members who had superior performances.

Preseason and In-Season Practice Format

The following format demonstrates the similarities and differences between preseason and in-season practices. In both cases, daily practices should never last more than two hours. After that point, scholastic wrestlers tend to lose their ability to concentrate.

• **Conditioning Warm-Up Exercises (10 to 15 minutes).** These exercises should stress total-body flexibility, strength, and endurance. Such training will help prevent injuries. The same warm-up should be used for both preseason and in-season practices.

• **Wrestling Drill Work (10 to 15 minutes).** Passive to active drills involving skills and moves from all facets of wrestling are the priority during this phase of practice. Use this approach in both preseason and in-season practice.

• **Step-by-Step Analysis of Wrestling Moves (10 to 15 minutes).** In this phase, thoroughly demonstrate moves, then let the wrestlers practice the maneuvers' essential parts step-by-step. Use this technique often in preseason practices but only when necessary during in-season practices.

- **Wrestling Workout Sessions (30 to 60 minutes).** The wrestling workout sessions should be much more intense during in-season practices, when wrestler conditioning is at its peak. Preseason workouts should last about 30 minutes; in-season wrestling workout sessions should last for nearly an hour. During this time, divide the wrestlers into groups. While one group is wrestling, the other group is running and weight training. Thus, no one is standing around while others are wrestling. (If your wrestlers do lift weights, it should be every other day.)

  During the wrestling workout sessions, you should frequently stop wrestlers in the middle of action with two purposes in mind. First, show the wrestlers how they are inadequately executing moves. Second, if necessary, demonstrate another move that would be more suitable for the same situation. Keep in mind, the wrestling workout sessions are the most important phase of in-season practices.

- **Conditioning Finish Exercises (10 to 15 minutes).** These end-of-practice exercises should be "snappy," with emphasis on strength and endurance skills. This phase would be identical for both preseason and in-season practices.

Never forget that as a coach, you are also a teacher. You should always entertain any responsible questions from your wrestlers regarding practice drills and moves. If a wrestler does not understand the significance of what he is doing, successful accomplishment of a maneuver will rarely be the result. The following are several teaching tips to ensure your practices are meaningful and produce winning results.

Teaching New Moves

When teaching a new move to your wrestlers, you should be able to do the maneuver flawlessly yourself. A step-by-step analysis of the move is your best approach. Emphasize those aspects of the maneuver that make it effective in competition.

Also, it is imperative that you stress *why* a move should be drilled in a certain manner, and what could happen if it is not. The more profound understanding your wrestlers have regarding the purpose behind each move, the easier it will be for them to master it.

The adept wrestling coach never attempts to demonstrate a move he does not fully understand. There is no shame in admitting to your wrestlers that you will need to do some research involving a certain wrestling skill. Your athletes will respect this course of action much more than if you feign knowledge of a move. In fact, you could easily harm your wrestlers' performance by showing a move you don't know authoritatively.

Avoiding Staleness

Staleness in practice may be defined as that time in the season when the wrestlers appear sluggish and seem to be regressing in their wrestling skills. This phenomenon usually occurs midway through the season. Two courses of action may be taken to alleviate the problem: First, give your wrestlers a day off from practice. This will revitalize their attitudes and focus their thoughts. Second, devote one practice to an activity the wrestlers will enjoy that is completely unrelated to wrestling. For example, they might play a game of crab soccer or have an arm-wrestling tournament during practice, and then be sent home for the day. (Refer to chapter 6 for additional conditioning activities for allaying staleness.)

Promoting Practice Cooperation and Competition

Cooperation and competition are both intricate aspects of a successful and productive wrestling program. Cooperation may take the form of the more experienced wrestlers helping novice wrestlers correctly drill the many wrestling skills that need to be learned. Also, various drills entail a cooperative effort, where one wrestler offers the proper resistance for correct drill performance.

Of course, the most important element for producing championship programs is practice competition. The more a wrestler is pushed in practice, the better he will perform in dual meets and tournaments. Without question, the promotion of a competitive spirit within your daily workout sessions can never be overemphasized.

I feel it is very difficult to distinguish the difference between cooperation and competition within the practice setting. When you have developed a competitive attitude in your team, each member will complement the others by exhibiting maximum effort at practice. In other words, two practice partners, competitively motivated, are cooperating with each other by pushing each other and striving to be the best.

Just as cooperation and competition are important factors in the classroom, the same should be true in the practice room as well. There are many classroom strategies and techniques that can and should be incorporated into your daily practice sessions. Your wrestling program must include the following:

- Well-structured practice plans
- Competent demonstrations of drilling moves by the coach
- Knowledge of how to combat practice staleness
- An understanding of the relationship between cooperation and competition within the realm of daily practices

Specialized Wrestling Workouts

The typical wrestling workout session involves spending about 50 percent of the time in the neutral position, perfecting takedown skills. This is an astute workout approach because takedown superiority is so important to winning matches. Next, both bottom and top mat wrestling would be equally divided for the purpose of polishing escape/reversal and ride/pinning combination skills.

Likewise, you will sometimes want to incorporate workouts that add variation to the traditional wrestling session, simply for a change of pace. Chain wrestling, situation wrestling, round-robin wrestling, and blindfold wrestling are excellent alternatives that are described in the following pages.

Chain Wrestling

Too often in contemporary scholastic matches the bottom wrestler will attempt to escape or reverse his opponent by using only one or two moves. If they don't work, his opponent ultimately ends up riding him. We seem to have forgotten a lost art—chain wrestling, a fast-paced bottom maneuver and top counter-maneuver wrestling activity. The most common chain wrestling skills include the following multiple moves:

Standard Chain Wrestling Workout

Step 1	Sit-out to turn-in (bottom wrestler)
	Follow sit-out to turn-in (top wrestler)
Step 2	Sit-out to turn-out (bottom wrestler)
	Follow sit-out to turn-out (top wrestler)
Step 3	Switch (bottom wrestler)
	Reswitch (top wrestler)
Step 4	Side roll (bottom wrestler)
	Re-side roll (top wrestler)
Step 5	Granby roll (bottom wrestler)
	Granby roll follow-through on head (top wrestler)
Step 6	Stand-up (bottom wrestler)
	Back heel trip to mat (top wrestler)

Wrestlers repeat this chain wrestling process as many times as instructed by the coach (usually three to five cycles) with wrestler W1 on the bottom. Then wrestler W2 would assume the bottom position, repeating the cycle the same number of times.

Of course, you may develop variations to this chain wrestling format to suit your particular mat wrestling concerns. No matter how you plan your chain wrestling activity, the key purpose of the workout is to train the bottom wrestler not to stop after one or two moves.

Another benefit of chain wrestling is that it teaches the top wrestler how to follow moves performed by the bottom wrestler. Likewise, it is a superb conditioning tool for workout sessions. You may even want to create a practice competition out of chain wrestling, timing the wrestlers to see which pair is quickest in completing the cycles.

In recent decades, coaches have placed so much emphasis on takedowns that many have ignored the importance of moving on the bottom. Chain wrestling is a snappy workout activity that doesn't take much practice time and leads to improved mat wrestling.

Situation Wrestling

Situation wrestling is usually incorporated during the season. It is much like a regular workout session with one exception: the wrestlers are placed in various wrestling positions and begin wrestling from that point. As with typical wrestling workouts, the coach should periodically stop the wrestlers to demonstrate what they are doing wrong.

There is a twofold purpose for including situation wrestling in daily practice sessions. First, you can use the strategy to work on new moves and to demonstrate how they should be performed during real wrestling situations.

The second rationale for adding situation wrestling to practice plans involves the scouting phase of coaching. While scouting rival teams, the coach often observes certain moves that members of these squads use the most to score points. Wisely, the coach will place his wrestlers in these various move situations, having them counter the maneuvers in preparation for an upcoming dual meet or tournament. This wrestling strategy has been very successful over the years.

Let's now consider two examples of situation wrestling—one for perfecting new moves and the other to prepare for competition.

Drilling a New Move

The coach has just completed demonstrating the standing suicide switch reversal maneuver. At this point, the wrestlers perform the maneuver in the following manner:

1. After standing up, the bottom wrestler fakes a standing switch, turning from one side to the other.
2. Then the bottom wrestler drops forward to the mat head first.
3. Finally, just before the bottom wrestler's head hits the mat, he executes a quick hip-heist switch, scoring the reversal.

After the wrestlers passively perform the move, the coach then places the wrestlers in the standing position and blows the whistle. With the top wrestler resisting fully, the bottom wrestler is given 15 seconds to complete the standing suicide switch. This is an all-out burst of wrestling effort by both wrestlers, with the coach periodically stopping the action to correct mistakes.

Drilling for Competition

When scouting the next dual meet opponent, the coach learns that the majority of wrestlers are very proficient at scoring double-leg takedowns.

At practices leading up to the meet, the coach places the wrestlers in the neutral position. He instructs the attacking team members to deeply penetrate the opponents' defense, clamping their hands around the knees.

On the whistle, the wrestlers defend themselves from the double-leg takedown counter, performing the following steps:

Step 1   Crossface and sprawl

Step 2   Whizzer and hip into opponent with whipping action

Step 3   Force head down with free hand and push away

This process continues until all practice partners have demonstrated the ability to properly counter the double-leg takedown.

Situation wrestling will greatly enhance the skill level of all team members. Do not fail to make it part of your workout repertoire.

Round-Robin Wrestling

Round-robin wrestling is another action-packed workout. One advantage to round-robin wrestling is that the entire squad participates simultaneously. This routine involves the following procedure:

1. Divide the team into groups of five wrestlers who weigh as close to each other as possible.

2. Assign a number from 1 to 5 to each wrestler in the group.

3. Wrestler 1 steps in the center of his group. He is given 30 seconds to score a takedown on each member of his group as follows:
   - Wrestler 1 vs. wrestler 2
   - Wrestler 1 vs. wrestler 3
   - Wrestler 1 vs. wrestler 4
   - Wrestler 1 vs. wrestler 5

4. If a takedown is scored in less than 30 seconds, the participants stand up and go at it again (and again) until time has expired.

5. Then wrestler 2 does the same with wrestlers 3, 4, 5, and 1. The process continues until everyone in the group has spent his time in the middle.

6. This round-robin session would include wrestling in the referee's position, emphasizing escapes, reversals, rides, or pinning combinations.

7. The inactive wrestlers for each group may act as spotters, protecting the active wrestlers from going out of bounds or colliding with other pairs.

As you can visualize, round-robin wrestling consists of a very invigorating workout. The prime objectives are quite obvious: conditioning and further skill development. Following are some interesting variations that make this alternative wrestling strategy even more intriguing:

1. Each group member as the primary wrestler would be required to counter maneuvers directed toward him by his round-robin rival, per covert instructions given to his practice opponents from the coach. This would encompass countermoves from both the neutral and referee's (bottom and top) positions.

2. The inactive wrestlers in the group could be instructed to run in place, rather than just stand there.

3. The coach could include an intragroup competition of the round-robin exercise by keeping track of who has the most takedowns (for example) in each group during the session workout. One appropriate incentive would be to exempt the winning wrestlers from closing exercises.

Of course, the creative coach may come up with even more novel approaches to enhance the round-robin experience. That's fantastic! Just remember to follow the previous guidelines, and it will be a productive and successful substitute to the traditional workout scheme.

Blindfold Wrestling

Blindfold wrestling is another beneficial practice innovation. The workout session is the same, with one exception: the wrestlers are blindfolded. Though the wrestlers may be a little hesitant at first, they will soon realize that they really don't need their eyes to wrestle.

Proper body positioning in wrestling is really a matter of feel, a sense of where you are or should be. Of course, such mat sense can be achieved only via years of practice. Blindfold wrestling is one workout medium a coach can implement to achieve this wrestler-oriented goal. The only props needed are blindfolds cut from old bed sheets. Following are a few basic guidelines for incorporating blindfold wrestling into your daily practices:

1. When first introducing the wrestlers to blindfold wrestling, blindfold only one of the wrestlers in each pair. The sighted wrestler will help stop his opponent when going out of bounds.

2. After both wrestlers have experienced being alternately blindfolded and feel comfortable with the technique, blindfold both of them.

3. To start in the neutral position, the two wrestlers will use the "finger-touch" method as described in Rule 6 of the *NFHS Wrestling Rules Book*. This will also prepare the wrestlers should they ever have to compete against a wrestler with a vision impairment.

4. No variations are needed for the referee's position, even if the optional offensive starting position is used.

5. The wrestlers must stay in continuous contact with each other throughout the entire workout.

Safety measures must be taken into consideration. First, there should be fewer wrestling pairs competing on the mats than usual during blindfold wrestling. Second, those wrestlers waiting to work out must act as spotters, stopping their peers as they are about to go out of bounds. Third, these wrestlers should also lead the blindfolded wrestlers back to their starting positions and restart them. Finally, the coach's whistle must be the signal for all blindfolded wrestlers to stop immediately.

During a blindfold wrestling session, the coach should stop the wrestlers and ask them what they are experiencing. The most common response will be that the wrestlers found themselves reacting to their opponents' movements rather than thinking about what to do.

You will learn by watching whether your wrestlers are responding properly and swiftly enough, relying primarily on their sense of touch rather than sight. And as we all know, this tactile (or mat) sense is a characteristic observed in all champion wrestlers.

Chain wrestling, situation wrestling, round-robin wrestling, and blindfold wrestling have so much to add to a comprehensive wrestling program. These workout alternatives increase stamina, develop continuous mat (or ground) wrestling abilities, improve takedown skills, promote mat sense, and further prepare the wrestlers for competition.

Off-Season Activities

The dedicated wrestler does not stop learning and training when the last practice of the season ends. He is continually looking for ways to improve his wrestling skills, muscle tone, and cardiovascular endurance. These objectives can be accomplished through a variety of activities during the postseason months. The following are off-season priorities for the aspiring state champion: summer wrestling clinics, postseason wrestling tournaments, weight training, and off-season sports or running.

Summer Wrestling Clinics

To improve technique, the sincere wrestler should attend summer wrestling clinics, prepared to take notes. He should not try to learn all the moves taught during the weeklong clinic, especially those so-called "clinic moves." These are maneuvers that look fancy but are rarely used or successful in competition. They are not founded on sound fundamentals. Clinicians present them to catch the eyes of the campers in order to teach the truly worthwhile moves.

The wrestler's prime objective should be to learn one or two new moves in each area of wrestling (takedowns, escapes/reversals, and rides/pinning combinations). They should be maneuvers that suit his wrestling style and body type. For example, if a wrestler is tall and thin, he should pay special attention to novel leg-wrestling moves.

Finally, the wrestler must consider the moves that he has had the most success with in past competitions. With this in mind, when the clinician demonstrates the wrestler's favorite moves, he should write down those subtle additions to the maneuver that make it even more effective in a match.

Clinics can be very worthwhile in perfecting wrestling skills if the clinic participant lives by the following two guidelines:

1. The wrestler must keep focused on the preceding suggestions.

2. The wrestler must approach the clinic as though it were a classroom. It is not to be perceived as a place for competition but as a place for learning. Therefore, he should never be afraid to ask questions!

In abiding by these guidelines, the wrestler will find the clinic experience to be of great personal benefit on the mats.

Postseason Wrestling Tournaments

Of course, there is no substitute for experience when it comes to developing wrestling skills. So if a wrestler is determined to be a state champion in today's highly competitive athletic world, he will need to compete in postseason tournaments.

On the other hand, there are some very important concerns that must be addressed regarding the advantages of postseason tournaments for the wrestler. Following are recommendations for participating in open wrestling competitions after the regular season:

1. First and foremost, the wrestler should join a well-coached wrestling club that stresses conditioning as well as the basics of the mat sport. The surest way to get seriously injured at a postseason tournament is not being in sound physical condition. It would be a tragedy to miss in-season action due to a long-term injury sustained at a postseason wrestling tournament.

2. The wrestler should *not* be concerned with weight reduction when competing in postseason tournaments. Year-round weight watching will lead to wrestling burnout. This loss-of-desire phenomenon has ended the careers of many fine wrestlers.

3. Do not wrestle in too many postseason tournaments. Five highly competitive wrestling tournaments would suffice. You don't want to peak at the end of summer but at the end of the wrestling season . . . at the state championships!

The wrestler's goal for wrestling in postseason tournaments should be threefold: First, he should continue to use successful moves previously learned in an effort to perfect them.

Second, this is the time of the year to attempt new moves. It doesn't cost the wrestler or his school's wrestling team anything if he fails to complete a new maneuver. The key is that the wrestler learns from the experience and makes the appropriate adjustments.

Finally, the wrestler should be constantly evaluating his progress with the assistance of his club coach. Summer wrestling tournaments must be viewed as a means to an end, preparing the wrestler for competitive action during the season.

Remember: college coaches pay far more attention to where you placed at states than where you placed in postseason tournaments.

Weight Training

The three prime components of successful wrestling are skill development, conditioning, and strength. When opposing wrestlers are identical in skill development and conditioning, the deciding factor often becomes strength.

Weight training is a year-round endeavor if a wrestler aspires to be a state champion. Furthermore, the wrestler's priority should be to lift weights for muscle endurance strength—more reps with less weight, and not for explosive strength—few reps with more weight (see chapter 6).

The wrestler's first step in initiating an off-season weight training program is to talk with his wrestling coach, strength coach, or weightlifting trainer from the local fitness center. One of these individuals will see to it that the wrestler starts his weight training program at appropriate weights (and with the correct amount of time at each station) for his body type. Not knowing the proper weight or number of sets and repetitions to do for beginning weight training can cause serious muscular injury.

One time-tested approach is circuit training with one set of 10 repetitions for each of three weightlifting exercise cycles. The amount of weight for each exercise should be enough that the wrestler strains to accomplish the last two or three repetitions. The ideal weight-training program should occur three days a week (for example, Monday, Wednesday, and Friday).

Safety is another important factor. To begin with, it would be wise to work with a partner of similar body size so that one can spot while the other is lifting. Note also the following basic safety tips for free weights and weightlifting machines.

Free Weights

1. Take great care in putting the weights on the bar evenly; otherwise the bar could tip, potentially causing injury.

2. Make sure all weights are locked securely.

3. Watch out for bars that are shoulder height or above. Athletes could get serious facial injuries by walking into the bar.

4. Put barbells, dumbbells, and weight plates away when you are finished so that nobody trips over them.

Weightlifting Machines

1. See to it that the selector keys are inserted all the way.

2. Place levers and seats at locations that suit your body size.

3. Establish a stable sitting and foot-support base when performing exercises.

4. Keep hands and fingers as far as possible from any moving objects on the weightlifting machine.

Always remember that off-season weight training is just as important to the dedicated wrestler as in-season weight training.

Off-Season Sports

A final concern for the wrestler in the off-season is to be actively involved in enhancing his cardiovascular endurance. This can be accomplished via many avenues of physical activity. We will begin with off-season sports.

In the spring, the wrestler could compete in track and field. The wrestler who is sincere about his physical endurance should compete in long-distance events, such as the 1500- or 3000-meter events.

Baseball is another great spring competition; it is outstanding for short sprint training but not for endurance workouts. Should a wrestler choose to play baseball, great! However, he should also consider doing extra running.

Two great autumn activities that are conducive to cardiovascular efficiency are cross-country and soccer. The diligent wrestler would be wise to compete in one of these two sports before wrestling season.

Finally, the most popular American sport of the fall—football—is another athletic prospect for the wrestler during the autumn months. Like baseball, this extremely physical sport also requires brief bursts of physical activity during competition, but not stamina. So the serious wrestler who plays football needs to add running to his daily routine.

Off-Season Running

If a wrestler is not competing in off-season sports that promote physical endurance, he must design his own running program (refer to chapter 6, page 205). Following is an off-season running plan that has worked for many champion wrestlers. It coincides with the weight-training schedule prescribed in the previous section.

Because the wrestler is lifting on Monday, Wednesday, and Friday, he should run on alternating days—Tuesday, Thursday, and Saturday. Sunday would be a day of rest. These recommendations will maximize the effectiveness of a running program:

1. The wrestler must first perform flexibility exercises for the legs and arms before running.

2. During the summer months, the wrestler should run in the mornings and carry water to beat the heat.

3. The wrestler should run four to six miles.

4. Interval training is an outstanding strategy for running. This method involves alternating running and sprinting. For example, the wrestler's initial pace could involve seven- to nine-minute miles, depending on his

body build. If in doubt, he should ask for his coach's advice. While running, the wrestler would sprint 30 seconds every two minutes, using a stopwatch. Substitutes for sprinting include running up hills or steps during the workout.

5. When the wrestler's run is completed, he should cool down by walking for 10 to 15 minutes. At this time, he should also hydrate himself by drinking enough water to make him feel comfortable.

Off-season activities are very important for wrestlers who want to succeed in the mat sport. Summer wrestling clinics, postseason wrestling tournaments, weight training, and off-season sports and running are prerequisites for such achievement. As their coach, you are responsible for guiding them in such a positive direction.

Conclusion

The key to a championship wrestling program is how well you organize your daily practice drill and workout sessions to fit the needs of your wrestlers. It is also up to you to develop and enact a well-rounded, yearlong strategy your wrestlers can follow. To use a movie-production metaphor, you are the producer, scriptwriter, and the director—do not let the actors down!

About the Editor

William A. Welker, EdD, boasts 50 years of experience as a successful wrestler, coach, and official. He is a former Pennsylvania Interscholastic Athletic Association (PIAA) state champion and two-time All-State wrestler. As head sophomore coach at Wheeling Park High School (West Virginia), he was instrumental in producing three AAA state championship teams. Since 1974, Welker has written nearly 500 articles on the art and science of wrestling and published a computer-assisted training manual for scholastic wrestling referees titled *Wrestling: Sports Officials Applied Skills and Knowledge Program*. He was selected as the National Wrestling Sportswriter of the Year by *Wrestling USA Magazine* in 1987, and he has been chosen as the West Virginia Wrestling Sportswriter of the Year an unprecedented five times by the state coaches' association.

Welker is a member of the Pennsylvania Sports Hall of Fame (Bernie Romanoski Chapter) and the Pennsylvania District IV Wrestling Hall of Fame. He has served as a clinician and rules interpreter for West Virginia since 1989. In 2001, he was honored as a Distinguished Official by the National Federation of State High School Associations, being one of only eight officials selected annually from all sports across the country. He was also named the 2002 National Wrestling Official of the Year.

Welker received both his bachelor's and master's degrees from the University of Pittsburgh. He later earned a doctorate in the field of education from West Virginia University. Welker and his wife, Peggy, have four children and 10 grandchildren. They reside on Wheeling Island in Wheeling, West Virginia.

About the Contributors

Jim Akerly is the founder, director, and coach for the Quest School of Wrestling in Canonsburg, Pennsylvania, where he has produced many prominent youth, scholastic, and collegiate wrestlers. While wrestling for West Virginia University, Akerly became the winningest wrestler in school history, recording 119 victories, and was a silver medalist at the prestigious Midlands Tournament in 1986. He qualified for the NCAA Division I Championships three times and earned All-American laurels in 1987. As a coach, Akerly headed up the Pennsylvania Freestyle and Greco national teams from 1989 to 1997. At the collegiate

level, he coached at West Virginia University, Edinboro (Pennsylvania), Rider University (New Jersey), the University of Virginia, and American University in Washington, DC. While coaching at American University, he was selected as the Colonial Athletic Association's Wrestling Coach of the Year in 1997. Akerly resides in Canonsburg, Pennsylvania.

Bill Archer is the assistant principal and head wrestling coach at Huntington High School (West Virginia), where his teams have amassed a phenomenal dual meet record of 426-83 (.837). Over the past 33 years, he has won 24 regional championships (which ranks him as one of the top 10 coaches in the state) and produced 25 individual West Virginia state champions. In 2001, this two-time state Coach of the Year was selected as the National Wrestling Coach of the Year by the National High School Coaches Association. A former West Virginia Secondary School Activities Commission

(WVSSAC) state champion, Archer was the all-time winningest wrestler at Marshall University in Huntington and was inducted into the university's Athletic Hall of Fame in 2004. Archer is the state editor for *Wrestling USA Magazine* and has served as the state chairman for USA Wrestling for the last 20 years. He holds a master's degree in educational administration. Archer and his wife, Diane, have two children and reside in Huntington, West Virginia.

Dave LaMotte is the head wrestling coach for the Salt River Pima-Maricopa Indian Community High School in Scottsdale, Arizona. During his 24-year coaching tenure, LaMotte has produced 17 individual state champions, 53 state place winners, 28 district titlists, and 3 high school All-Americans. LaMotte began his coaching career at his high school alma mater in Bridgeport, Ohio, where his 1988 team captured the Division III State Championship and he was voted the Ohio Division III Coach of the Year in 1989. In 1993 LaMotte earned Coach of the Year honors when his Gilbert High School (Arizona) squad won the 5A State Championship. LaMotte also coached his two sons, who were both Arizona state champions and NCAA Division II All-Americans. As a competitor, LaMotte was an all-state high school wrestler and compiled a record of 103-14-2 for West Liberty State College (West Virginia). He was also a two-time National Association of Intercollegiate Athletics (NAIA) All-American and an NAIA champion. In 2004, he was inducted into West Liberty State College's Athletic Hall of Fame. LaMotte and his wife, Vickie, reside in Gold Canyon, Arizona.

Pat Pecora has served as the head wrestling coach for the University of Pittsburgh, Johnstown Campus, since 1976. During this time his squads have compiled a 365-103-3 (.775) dual-meet record, capturing 17 NCAA Division II east regional championships and two NCAA Division II national titles (1996 and 1999). Pecora has produced 100 All-Americans and 62 academic All-Americans, and seven of his wrestlers advanced to win a combined 13 national championships. Pecora has served two terms as president of the NCAA Division II Wrestling Coaches Association (NWCA), including 10 years as the NCAA Division II representative to the NWCA. He is a 10-time NCAA Division II East Regional Coach of the Year and two-time NCAA Division II National Coach of the Year (1995 and 1999). In 1999 he also received the NWCA's Coaching Excellence Award. Pecora is a member of five halls of fame, including the NCAA Division II and Pennsylvania

Wrestling Coaches Halls of Fame. As a wrestler at West Liberty State College (West Virginia), Pecora was a three-time All-West Virginia Conference selection and qualified for nationals twice. Pecora, his wife, Tracy, and their four children live in Johnstown, Pennsylvania.

Edwin C. Peery is a professor and coach emeritus for the United States Naval Academy. He was head coach of the Midshipmen wrestling team from 1960 until 1987 and retired from the Academy in 2000. During his coaching tenure, Peery posted a 311-90-14 dual-meet record, coaching eight Eastern Intercollegiate Wrestling Association (EIWA) championship teams, 48 individual EIWA titlists, and 16 NCAA All-Americans. He was named NCAA Coach of the Year in 1968 and received EIWA coaching honors in 1974 and 1986. He is an honorary lifetime member of the National Wrestling Coaches Association, having served as its president and as a member of its rules committee. A two-time Pennsylvania Interscholastic Athletic Association (PIAA) state champion, Peery won three NCAA titles under the coaching of his father, the legendary Rex Peery, at the University of Pittsburgh. Peery is also a distinguished member of the National Wrestling Hall of Fame and the Pennsylvania Wrestling Coaches Hall of Fame, and he was selected as an Outstanding American by the Maryland chapter of the National Wrestling Hall of Fame. Peery and his wife, Gretchen, reside in West River, Maryland.

Ken L. Taylor has been head wrestling coach at Rocky Mountain High School in Fort Collins, Colorado, since 2001. During this time, he has led teams to win two regional championships and one district tournament as well as produced three state champions. An outstanding coach and official at both the college and high school levels over the last 30 years, Taylor was also a 1972 NAIA All-American silver medalist for Colorado's Adams State College and captain of the school's 1972 NAIA National Championship team. During Taylor's 25-year coaching tenure at Poudre High School (Colorado), his teams won four district titles and two regional championships. He also produced seven top 10 teams at the state level, six individual state titlists, and two state runner-up squads. In 1981 he was voted Colorado State Wrestling Coach of the Year, and he coached the Colorado Wrestling All-Star Team in 1981 and 1990. Taylor, his wife, Julie, and stepson reside in Fort Collins, Colorado.

Craig Turnbull has served as the head wrestling coach at West Virginia University for 26 years. He is the winningest coach in West Virginia University history, having built one of the strongest and most dominating wrestling programs in the United States. His teams have compiled an impressive record of 221-148-6, producing 18 Eastern Wrestling League (EWL) champions, 16 All-Americans, and 3 wrestlers who won five NCAA Division I titles. Since winning the NCAA Division I Rookie Coach of the Year award, Turnbull's squads have consistently placed in the top 25 nationally. In 1990, Turnbull was selected as the Eastern Wrestling League's Coach of the Year as West Virginia University captured its first Eastern Mat Poll number-one ranking. Turnbull was also selected to coach the National Wrestling Coaches Association's All-Star Classic in 1992. He has been named the EWL's Coach of the Year three times and has won five Eastern Dual Meet Championships from 1990 to 2003. He is currently a board member of the National Wrestling Coaches Association. Turnbull, his wife, Sue, and their two children reside in Morgantown, West Virginia.

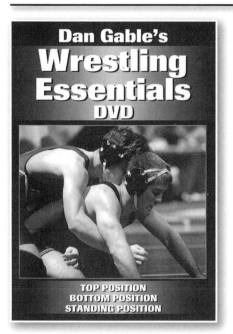
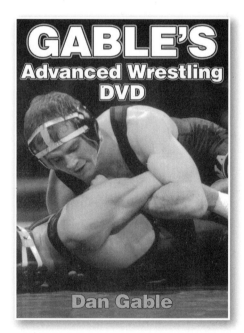